A Brief for Belief:
The Case for Catholicism

A Brief for Belief:
The Case for Catholicism

by Frederick W. Marks

Queenship

PUBLISHING COMPANY
P.O. Box 220 • Goleta, CA 93116
(800) 647-9882 • (805) 692-0043 • Fax: (805) 967-5843

To Sylvia

Ad majorem Dei gloriam

Library of Congress Number # 99-76002

Published by:
    Queenship Publishing
    P.O. Box 202
    Goleta, CA 93116
    (800) 647-9882 • (805) 692-0043 • Fax: (805) 967-5843

Printed in the United States of America

ISBN: 1-57918-114-7

Acknowledgments

Most books are a collaborative effort, and this one is no exception. Wherever possible, I have cited published sources. But I should like, in addition, to acknowledge the support of those who took the time to read preliminary drafts of the *Brief*: Fr. Kenneth Baker, S.J., Professor Warren Carroll, and Rev. C. John McCloskey III; likewise, those who offered detailed suggestions on content and style and whose interpretive leanings may not always have coincided with my own (one a Protestant minister, another a Jewish rabbi who wishes to remain anonymous): Fr. Avery Dulles, S.J., George Sim Johnston, Rev. Bruce Metzger, Charles Scribner III, Dennis Shea, Reverend Robert D. Smith, Rev. Peter Stravinskas, and Fr. James Torrens, S.J.

Above all, I am grateful to my wife, Sylvia, who listened to innumerable oral "presentations" and read an equal number of drafts with the eye of an English professor and the soul of a sweetheart.

"You shall know the truth and the truth shall make you free."

— Jesus of Nazareth (John 8:32)

Table of Contents

Preface

The instant we detect a threat to our physical well-being, we act. Whatever the doctor, lawyer, or broker advises, we do. Yet in the spiritual realm, where proposals based on a wide range of knowledge and experience can heal both soul and body, we tend to coast, unable or unwilling to admit a state of helplessness. On the one hand, we gladly undergo the most painful surgery to prolong life on earth by a handful of years. On the other, we shrink from religious conversion.

Why so? Do we fear the loss of human respect? "Men ... can seldom discern even the simplest and most obvious truth," wrote Leo Tolstoy, "if it be such as obliges them to admit the falsity of conclusions they have formed, perhaps with much difficulty — conclusions of which they are proud, which they have taught to others, and on which they have built their lives."[1] Are we wedded to the conventional wisdom because we have opted for a certain way of life? The late Archbishop Fulton Sheen used to say that, "if you do not live the way you think, you will soon come to think the way you live." Such words are as sobering as they are true, for worldliness, like alcohol or tobacco, is a narcotic; and just as compulsive smokers and those in the early stages of alcoholism will swear that they are in complete control, so, too, do men and women of the world experience a false sense of security. Ask them about the state of their soul, and they reply nonchalantly that they have not given it a thought since childhood. And who among us does not fit this description in one way or another? All of us are frail.

---

[1] From the 1886 treatise, "What is Art?"

We all cling to the things of earth and crave consolation in the here and now. Temptation is the lot of every man.

The good news is that worldliness, like compulsive drinking and smoking, is a habit that can be broken. Detoxification of the soul may not be easy. It may require humility and courage. Still, it is possible. Indeed, I should not have written the following essay if I did not view spiritual liberation as well within the reach of anyone willing to enlist in an honest search for truth, goodness, and beauty.

Such a search is what this book is all about. Some may come to it without very much experience in religion. Others may have had religious experience, but not of a positive kind. Still others may belong to some group outside the Catholic fold. Perhaps their curiosity has gotten the better of them. Finally, there may be Catholics who have come to the *Brief* for a bit of timely reinforcement, sensing correctly that faith is a perishable commodity. To all of you, as well as to those who merely wish to argue the case, I say, "Right on. This is your ticket!"

Frederick W. Marks
Forest Hills, NY
March 1999

Chapter I

The Case for God

*The Infinite and the Eternal are as essential for man
as the little planet on which he dwells.*

Fyodor Dostoyevsky

No amount of debunking by the world's cleverest critics, from
skeptics of the Italian Renaissance to French revolutionaries and
Russian communists, has been able to extinguish belief in the hereafter. Religion has been a fixture of human society since time immemorial and from one end of the globe to the other. An English
bishop in 1736 deplored the fact that a great many of his country-
men had come to regard Christianity as fictitious, and a generation
or two later, the writer Horace Walpole would speak of going to
Rome to witness the election of the "last pope."[2] Yet Christianity
in general, and the papacy in particular, goes marching on.

Although science seemed to shake the foundations of faith
during the nineteenth century and God was pronounced "dead" on
a number of occasions, the twentieth century proved to be the most
spectacular of all eras for evangelization. In 1938, a German en-
voy to the coronation of Pius XII echoed Walpole's jest: "A beautiful ceremony, but unfortunately the last."[3] Hitler, had he lived to
hear the conciliatory, almost apologetic, tone of Mikhail Gorbachev

---

[2] John McManners, ed., *The Oxford Illustrated History of Christianity* (1990),
     282 (on Bishop Butler).
[3] *Our Sunday Visitor*, November 23, 1997, p. 14.

of the Soviet Union on a trip to the Vatican half a century later, would have been astonished. As would Marx and Lenin. For seventy-five years, the Kremlin employed every device imaginable to destroy belief in a divine being. All the levers of state power, ranging from economic inducements to media indoctrination, were pressed into service. But to no avail. The "new" Soviet man proved worse than a failure, and by 1990, it was clear that atheistic communism had suffered a signal defeat.

During the 1920s, the president of Mexico set, as his goal, "the uprooting of religion." Thereafter, many Mexican states closed down practically every Catholic church within their jurisdiction. No Catholic was allowed to teach in the schools, and faith seemed a relic of the past. Few could have imagined that by 1997, there would be more young men studying for the priesthood in Guadalajara, Mexico's second largest city, than in any other metropolis in the world — over a thousand.[4]

Doubtless, one of the reasons why religion has proven so durable is that it leads to health and happiness. Saints have written convincingly of ecstasy: atheists never. Some of the world's most brilliant men and women have surrendered their lives rather than deny the faith that empowered them. How utterly filled with joy they must have been to choose martyrdom over apostasy!

History attests to the fact that those who break with God are likely to be unhappy even in this world. The most irreligious century of modern times, the twentieth, is noted for behavior that is positively bestial, with family breakup occurring at a rate previously unimaginable. Mankind has been engulfed by the millions in deadly class warfare. At the same time, skyrocketing statistics on crime, suicide, illegitimacy, and abortion form a regular litany of social anguish in the principal centers of power.[5] Yale sociologist

---

[4] Human Life International *Special Report* #155 (November 1997), p. 2.

[5] According to an 846-page French academic study titled *The Black Book of Communism* (1997), Communist leaders were responsible for the deaths of somewhere between seventy-five and a hundred million people: In China 45-72 million; in the former USSR 20; in Cambodia 1.3-2.3 (million); North Korea 2; Africa 1.7; Afghanistan 1.5; Vietnam 1; Eastern Europe 1; and Latin America 150,000. See the *Wall Street Journal*, December 15, 1997, p. 22.

Neil Bennett concluded in 1988 that cohabiting couples (living in open defiance of the standard set by all the world's great religions) were 80% more likely to break up, either through separation or a subsequent divorce, than couples who had not lived together before marriage. Coincidentally, a U.S. Department of Health and Human Services study of more than 600,000 children the same year found the obvious: that youngsters living with a never-married or divorced mother were substantially more likely to cause trouble at school and to experience emotional problems.[6]

In the realm of health, there is a special price to be paid for flouting religious norms. Chemical abuse leads to cancer and sclerosis of the liver, while sexual immorality can bring on venereal disease and AIDS. Conversely, penitential fasting of the kind prescribed for the soul can work wonders on the physical plane as well because it removes toxins from the body. Studies show that regular churchgoers live longer and have fewer heart attacks, along with a lower incidence of hypertension, arteriosclerosis, and high blood pressure.[7] It can be shown, in addition, that older people who attend church services regularly are healthier and less liable to despair than those who don't.[8]

Religion, War, and Hypocrisy

Health and happiness notwithstanding, objections to belief in God are legion. It is claimed, in the first instance, that religion is divisive and a cause of war. On the face of it, this seems plausible enough. Yet politics, too, is divisive and a cause of war. So, too, is patriotism. Nor should one forget romance, with its cry of "all is fair in love and war." But how many would want to do away with

---

[6]   Margaret Thatcher, *Path to Power*, 552 (on U.S. Health Department statistics).
[7]   *The New York Times*, November 4, 1997 ("Science Watch"); *Catholic Digest*, February 1992, pp. 1-2.
[8]   See, for religion and health, *International Journal of Psychiatry in Medicine*, vol. 27, No. 3, 1997, pp. 234 and 247; also H. G. Koenig, *Research on Religion and Aging* (1995) and *Is Religion Good for Your Health?* (1997); *Journal of Behavioral Medicine*, 1978, 1 (1):37-43; *Journal of Religion and Health*, 1989, 28:265-78; *Journal of Chronic Disease*, 1972, 25:665-72; *American Journal of Public Health*, 1997, 87:957-61.

political parties, love of country, or marriage? Furthermore, how does one account for the fact that the most cynical century on the books is also the bloodiest, stained as it is by wholesale torture, mass murder, and genocide? Civil strife and international contention have exceeded all limits. Since 1945 alone, two hundred wars have claimed the lives of twenty million civilians. Evidently, if man does not fight in the name of religion, he will do so in the name of something else. Modern crusades are fought under the banners of nationalism, democracy, and communism.

Did Buddha, Jesus, or Mohammed seek to win converts by the sword? Moslems may have resorted to religious coercion, but they did so in spite of the express prohibition of such tactics by Islam's holy book, the Koran. Christians, too, have been known to override the gospel. Ultimately, it would seem that the question in a nutshell is this: What causes strife of *any* kind? How explain wrangling between husband and wife, father and son, mother and daughter-in-law? Clearly, man is prone to fight, and while he may do so in the name of God, it is simplistic to take him at his word. If anything, religion has been a mitigating factor. Spiritual leaders are normally on the side of arms control, disarmament, and mediation. Conflicts have been settled by the intervention of the papacy, and during the Middle Ages, the Church was successful in limiting the duration, as well as the scope, of armed conflict.

Along another line, one hears it said that as soon as believers leave their places of worship, they behave just as viciously, if not more so, than their agnostic friends. Again, there may be an element of truth in this, but as a general rule, it is belied by Gallup polls which indicate that churchgoers give four times as much to charity as non-churchgoers per household. They volunteer twice as much of their time on an individual basis, are twice as likely to donate to non-religious charities, and are a good deal less likely to cheat on their income tax (*The New York Times*, 4/20/91, p. 10).

Study after study by behavioral scientists suggests that religious belief is without peer as a remedy for social ills. Alcohol abuse is 300% higher among non-churchgoers, according to a University of California survey. By the same token, states with a larger religious affiliation have fewer homicides and suicides. A study by researchers at the University of Nevada demonstrates a key difference between Black males who wind up in prison and those who don't: the former either never went to church or stopped going at about the age of ten.

One can go further. The rate of divorce among regular churchgoers is 2%, and if such attendees engage in regular Bible reading, the figure drops to an astounding one half of 1%.[9] Moreover, when marital separation does occur, reconciliation rates are higher among regular churchgoers and higher still when both spouses are religiously observant.[10]

Religion as a Crutch

A third argument popular among non-believers portrays religion as a "crutch" designed for weaklings unable to shift. "Rugged individualists," as the saying goes, "can stand on their own two feet." Perhaps. But again, one must look at the record. Studies of the effect of Nazi concentration camps on inmates suggest that those who were religiously motivated had the best chance by far of withstanding pain and deprivation.

The "crutch" argument is doubly misleading insofar as it makes religion appear comfortable. Belief in God may console, but it also involves risk-taking. It places one under constraint. Christians, for example, view themselves as crucified to the world and the world to them, to quote St. Paul; and crucifixion is not a pleasant thing. Although religion brings joy, the cost on other counts is likely to be steep. Those preoccupied with the avoidance of pain are thus more likely to turn to panaceas such as free love, abortion, and euthanasia.

The American film industry has made something of a cult of "rugged individualism" sans God. John Wayne, in one of his best-known films, *The Sands of Iwo Jima*, plays an intrepid Marine. As he is about to go into battle, his girlfriend of the moment promises to pray for him, and he shoots back, "Let's not get religion!" Another all-time favorite, *High Noon*, casts Gary Cooper as a loner

---

9   *Catholic Digest*, August 1994, p. 79.
10   American Family Association *Journal*, April 1996, p. 9 (hereafter AFA *Journal*).

protecting a small town from outlaws. Like Wayne, Cooper is handsome and brave. But when the camera pans in on Sunday church services, our hero is conspicuously absent. What is more, a timid minister and equally timid congregation decline to lend a hand when the clock strikes twelve.

Wayne and Cooper come across as magnificent human beings. One cannot help wondering, however, if such individuals are not largely a figment of Hollywood's imagination. History is full of rugged individualists. Some, like Abraham Lincoln, Charles de Gaulle, and Winston Churchill were believers. Others, like Robespierre, Adolf Hitler, and Fidel Castro, were not. And there is a difference in terms of how they treated their fellow man. To be sure, we have all known atheists and agnostics who appear to be naturally good. But how many of them, on closer examination, turn out to have had parents, grandparents, or friends who were God-fearing and whose values may have rubbed off on them?

Maximilian Kolbe, who volunteered to give his life in exchange for that of a family man at Auschwitz, was a rugged individualist who happens at the same time to have been a priest. How many Kolbes have there been in the annals of atheism? Paul Johnson and E. Michael Jones have documented the shocking cruelty and callousness of leaders reputed to be hard-core cynics, men of the stripe of Voltaire, Marx, and Sartre.[11]

There is also the question of how the good pagan or "secular saint" transmits a personal code of conduct to succeeding generations if there is no book on which to rely and nothing more solid institutionally than a fraternal lodge. Can norms of morality be handed down from father to son and mother to daughter solely on the basis of individual preference and example? Arnold Toynbee was on the mark when he observed that "practice unsupported by belief is a wasting asset."[12] In the words of George Washington, "Reason and experience both forbid us to expect that national morality can prevail in exclusion of religious principle."[13]

---

[11] Paul Johnson, *Intellectuals*; E. Michael Jones, *Degenerate Moderns*.

[12] Quoted in Guhin, *John Foster Dulles*, 126.

[13] He also said that "of all the dispositions and habits which lead to political prosperity, religion and morality are indispensable supports."

The Problem of Pain

Finally, there are those who reject the notion of an all-knowing, all-loving, and all-powerful God on the assumption that it cannot be squared with so much in the world that appears ugly. "I can never believe in a God who would countenance the Nazi Holocaust," one is apt to hear. From an emotional point of view, this is perfectly understandable. But the person who makes such a statement must consider whether the mere existence of suffering — any kind of suffering — automatically precludes the possibility of a loving deity. Are we depressed or scandalized by the bawling of a hungry infant? No, because the child is presumed to have a bright future. Why, then, should the same principle not apply to adults? For believers, life on earth is but a microscopic speck on the screen of eternity, and all who behave themselves in this world can look forward to a bright future in the next.

It may seem unfair to equate the temporary suffering of a youngster experiencing gastrointestinal pain with Hitler's crime of genocide. Nevertheless, suffering either precludes the existence of God or it doesn't. One cannot very well draw a line between degrees of suffering or types of motivation, and to assume that man's cruelty toward his fellow man in the case of the Holocaust rules out the governance of divine providence is to hold God responsible for man's abuse of the precious gift of freedom, an abuse that does not go unpunished in the long run.

Even those who view pain as evil will allow that it can have good effects. Without pain as a warning, appendicitis would be fatal. And without occasional stiffness of joints and muscles, we would exercise to our detriment.

Then, too, the Bible tells us that suffering is just as apt to be a mark of God's special favor as it is a punishment: "Those whom the Lord loves he chastises" (Hebrews 12:6). One is reminded of the Jewish proverb, "What soap is to the body, tears are to the soul," which is borne out in so many ways. The sweetest and most empathetic persons are generally those who have been tested because suffering exalts the soul while prosperity and sustained ease tend to pull it down. Why is self-sacrifice the only road to success in scholarship, athletics, and business? Why does every major undertaking, from childbirth to the passing of a bar exam, entail struggle?

Beyond this, Christians believe they participate in the divine work of redemption by offering up everyday trials and tribulations. In this way, they are able to transform what is perceived by most as negative into something positive, even rejuvenating. The man who is not afraid to suffer is stronger than one who is, and the man or woman who welcomes pain, viewing it as salutary when offered up, will be stronger still. Christian saints have gone so far as to pray for adversity, regarding it as one of God's choicest blessings, and prospective converts have been known to find Christian theology so potent in this regard that it forces their hand. All of the greatest religions offer some form of consolation to suffering souls. But Christianity has a handle that is unique by virtue of the fact that, theologically speaking, Jesus fashioned suffering and death into instruments of salvation.

Without question, we are in the presence of mystery. But why should mystery stand in the way of belief? If God is what he is supposed to be, infinitely superior to us, we can no more grasp the inner workings of his grand design than a two-year-old can appreciate the need for parental discipline. Mystery should no more rule out belief in the hereafter than unanswered questions of a more practical nature rule out belief in science. Does the chemical engineer know how many elementary particles there are, or how the DNA molecule governs the development of a new-born baby? Can we explain magnetism, electricity, light, or gravity? Who knows why we spend one-third of our lives in a state of dormancy? Who can say how plants absorb energy from the sun in photosynthesis? Why do pole beans and other vines twist counterclockwise in the northern hemisphere the way water swirls down a drain (the Corioli effect)? Someone will say: because of the turning of the earth. But this does not explain why.

What is intelligence? One can define it by comparison; but can one say what it consists of? Studies of the brains of idiots and geniuses show no discernible difference in tissue or the way brain waves travel. Why, after so many centuries, is childbirth still attended by acute pain and anxiety? Why, despite the best effort of chemists, biologists, and medical technicians, do people of the present age die at exactly the same rate they died at the time of Moses: 100%. Granted, there have been fluctuations in longevity. But they pale by comparison with the iron law of decay and death.

In short, there is much that science cannot explain; yet we respect scientists. Should religion be treated any differently?

Design, Cause, and Effect

We have examined some of the standard objections to belief in God and found them wanting. But we can go further, indeed we *must* go further, since the burden of proof lies with the affirmative.

Not surprisingly, there are as many arguments *for* as *against* the existence of a Creator who is both omniscient and omnipotent, and the first of these derives from the principle of cause and effect: to wit, that for every effect there is a cause, for every motion a mover, and if we push the chain of causality all the way back to the beginning of time, we will arrive at a First Cause or Prime Mover, which is simply another name for God. One must assume, of course, that the world, as we know it, is not itself God and that it had a beginning. But since there was a time, according to anthropologists, when human beings did not exist, and since lower forms of life do not produce higher forms (i.e., no effect is greater than its cause), how could such an objection hold?

The axiom that a cause may be judged by its effect has many applications. Take the Bible, for example. Students of literature and observers of human nature believe it to be in a class by itself, vastly superior to any other work. And what does this, in turn, indicate about the credentials of its author?

God's handiwork in the order of natural creation is similarly suggestive. The grandeur of summer sunset and the splendor of fall foliage bespeak a font of sublime wisdom and majesty. Who but God could ever have ordained that no human fingerprint, no human face, and no human voice would ever be exactly the same as any other? Who but the Almighty could have formed every snowflake with a unique geometric configuration?

Is it an accident that the moon, 410 times smaller than the sun, is also 410 times closer to the earth, making possible a perfect eclipse? Who can explain the uncanny precision of planetary motion without postulating a supernatural blueprint? Who wrote the laws of the universe? How does the body recuperate from wounds? Is it coincidental that shrubs and trees maintain their symmetry? Or that nature delivers the precise mix of moisture and aridity needed for the sustenance of life? How awesome this world of ours! Who but an engineer with surpassing ability could have masterminded it all and brought it into being?

The teleological principle — namely, that everything in life, however large or small, has a purpose — is daily brought home to us by the findings of science, ecology in particular. It would seem logical, therefore, to assume that all of man's deepest longings, whether they be for beauty, justice, love, or lasting peace, must be capable of finding satisfaction in the hereafter. Likewise when it comes to our craving for moral and intellectual refinement. Just as one can tell that locomotives were made for rails, cars for the road, and ships for the sea, human beings who have fought the good fight appear to be headed for a heavenly reward. Conversely, the intensity and scope of evil — so far beyond the power of civil law to punish and at the same time so abhorrent to our sense of justice — is utterly inexplicable without positing the existence of purgatory and hell.

The Argument from Culture

Before proceeding to the next stage of our inquiry and probing the case for Christianity, there is one other train of thought with a claim to our attention since it is as neglected in the current literature as it is intriguing: namely, the correlation between spiritual conviction, on the one hand, and cultural achievement on the other.

Beginning with the field of letters and literature, historians tell us that religion was the driving force behind the spread of books, as well as the foundation of libraries and universities. We also know that college curricula during the period 1100-1800 were predominantly theological and that the world's best-loved authors have been God-fearing. Dante (a Third Order Franciscan), Shakespeare, Milton, and Bunyan head the list.

Frequent reference to the gods is found in Homer's *Odyssey* and Virgil's *Aeneid*. And this is true of mythological lore in general, not to mention classic Greek tales. Theseus prays before dispatching the Minotaur; Ulysses invokes the name of Zeus; and God is featured in Aesop's fable, "Jupiter and the Bee." The principal Greek and Roman historians were moralists of the highest order, men of the stamp of Herodotus, Thucydides, Livy, and Tacitus.[14] Emperor Augustus, patron of Virgil, Livy, and Horace, ushered in the golden age of Roman culture — the Augustan Age, as it is known — and he was notably pious. Soon after the death of Augustus, Rome abandoned its religion, and following in the footsteps of Greece four centuries earlier, its culture declined as artists relied increasingly on sex and violence.

The nineteenth century is especially rich in examples. Jane Austen had a father and two brothers who were clergymen. The Brontë sisters were also born in a parsonage. Harriet Beecher Stowe, who counted nine preachers in her immediate family — a father, seven brothers, and a husband — once said of her novel, *Uncle Tom's Cabin*, the most influential and widely read work of its kind ever published in the United States, "I did not write it. God wrote the book. I merely did His dictation."[15]

Alfred Lord Tennyson believed that "more things are wrought by prayer than this world dreams of," and Charles Dickens, England's premier novelist, regarded the New Testament as "the best book that ever was or ever will be." Dickens' tribute was genuine. He put a copy of the Gospels in the trunk of his youngest son when the latter set off for boarding school. He also wrote *A History of Our Lord Jesus Christ* for his children, and one of the themes of his *Child's History of England* is the power and presence of God. Henry VIII comes off as "one of the most detestable villains that ever drew breath."

Some, like Henrik Ibsen and Leo Tolstoy, started out as wayward youths. But once they brought their conduct into conformity with divine law, they came into their own, and the quality of their work soared. Ignatius of Loyola and Augustine began the same way, as moral mediocrities who, after undergoing spiritual rebirth, were able to tap into the titanic energy of God in a way that the

---

14 On Livy, see Sélincourt edition of his *Early History of Rome* (1960), 13.
15 Quoted by Alfred Kazan in *God and the American Writer* (1997).

world will never forget. Dostoyevsky spent six months in prison and was standing before a firing squad when a last-minute reprieve arrived. Only after hard labor and conversion to Christianity did he write *Crime and Punishment*, *The Idiot*, *The Possessed*, and *The Brothers Karamazov*.

Music

With Richard Wagner, it was the reverse. Wagner formed an adulterous attachment late in life. But by then, he had composed all of his major works, including the *Ring* cycle, which was cobbled together earlier than the date of its first performance would suggest. Music and literature tell much the same story.

Brahms' "Lullaby" is probably the most tender piece of its kind ever written, Schubert's "Ave Maria" the most touching of all songs, Handel's *Messiah* the world's most powerful oratorio, and all three were the work of men steeped in religious conviction. Handel, on completing the "Halleluia Chorus," confided to his servant, "I did think that I did see all heaven before me and the great God himself!" And when a nobleman remarked to him, "Sir, you have created in your *Messiah* a very entertaining work," he shot back, "I should be sorry if I only entertained them: I wish to make them better."

Efforts by managers of stage and screen to present Wolfgang Amadeus Mozart as lewd and frivolous are at best misguided. If he was remarkable for anything other than musical wizardry, it was for his piety. The day his beloved mother died was "the most melancholy" of his life, he confessed, but "God has called her to Himself ... The Lord giveth, and the Lord taketh away."[16]

At the age of twenty-two and already in full command of his powers, he conducted a concert in Paris. "I prayed to God that it might go well," he recalled, "for all is to His greater honor and glory." And after performing brilliantly, he reported that he "went off in my joy to the Palais Royal where I took a good ice, told over my beads [said the rosary] as I had vowed, and went home, where

---

[16] Wallace, trans., *The Letters of Wolfgang Amadeus Mozart, 1769-1791*, I, 209 (7/3/78); also I, 107.

I am always happiest."[17] In another instance, he speaks of meeting "a very honorable and kind man, but unhappily devoid of all religion ... Friends who have no religion cannot long be our friends."[18]

Clues to the character of an individual regarded by many as unsurpassed in musical genius are scattered throughout his letters. For example: "I must give you a piece of intelligence that you perhaps already know — namely that the ungodly arch-villain Voltaire has died miserably just like a brute. This is his reward." And again: "I have a project in my head for the success of which I daily pray to God. If it be His Almighty will, it must come to pass; but, if not, I am still contented."[19] In still another missive, he observes, "People say that I am ... polite and praise my manners."[20]

Mozart could have set up housekeeping with a girlfriend prior to marriage. But he declined: "I cannot live as many other young men do. In the first place, I have too great a sense of religion, too much love of my neighbor to do so, and too high a feeling of honor to deceive any innocent girl."[21] He attended daily Mass, and when he did take a wife, after postponing marriage with the express intention of developing his God-given talent, she was a professional singer who proved to be a devoted life-long companion.[22] "Previous to our marriage, he told his father, "we had for some time past attended Mass together as well as confessed and taken Holy Communion."[23]

Several years later, impoverished and in poor health, Mozart wrote, "I never lie down at night without thinking that [young as I am] I may be no more before the next morning dawns. And yet not one of all those who know me can say that I ever was morose or melancholy ... I daily thank my Creator for such a happy frame of mind and wish from my heart that every one of my fellow creatures may enjoy the same."[24] Six years later, at the age of thirty-

---

[17] Ibid., I, 212-14.
[18] Ibid., I, 160-61 (2/2/78).
[19] Ibid., I, 214 (7/3/78).
[20] Ibid., I, 273 (10/26/78).
[21] Ibid., letter for December 15, 1781.
[22] Ibid., II, 60 (7/25/81).
[23] Ibid., II, 145 (8/17/82).
[24] Ibid., II, 222.

five and hard pressed to support a growing family, he died and was laid to rest.

Franz Joseph "Papa" Haydn, father of the symphony, string quartet, and piano trio, was raised by a woman who wanted her son to be a priest. Geiringer, his biographer, describes him as "always ... deeply religious." All his compositions were written in praise of God, and all end with the words "Laus Deo."[25] Whenever he felt his inspiration lagging, he would rise from the piano and finger his beads.[26] Once, when asked how he was able to write so many pieces of supremely high quality, he explained, "I get up early, and as soon as I have dressed, I go down on my knees and pray God and the Blessed Virgin that I have another successful day."[27] Toward the end of his life, he is reported to have spent hours at a time praying the rosary.[28]

It is fitting that Haydn should have had Ludwig van Beethoven as a pupil. Not much material is available on Beethoven's interior life. What little we know, however, is revealing. Son of a serious Catholic mother, he lived a life that can only be described as militantly didactic. Around the edge of his writing table were to be found quotations on the existence of God, each of them in his own hand and neatly framed; and when he was about to die, he was insistent on having the ministrations of a priest.[29] Chided by one of his biographers for "moral priggishness," he is alleged to have protested a waitress' coquettish ways by boxing her ears. Here was a man who objected to the opera, *Don Giovanni*, on account of the dubious character of its protagonist. And, on discovering that his brother Johann's relationship with a live-in housekeeper had become grist for gossip, he applied to the bishop and then to the police to have the woman deported (a date was actually set for her departure; but Johann, not to be denied, promptly married the object of his affection).[30]

---

25 Ibid., 144; Geiringer biography (1946), 144.
26 Geiringer biography, 144.
27 Rosemary Hughes, *Haydn* (1962), 47.
28 Ibid., 106.
29 Bekker biography (1912), 55.
30 Schauffler biography (1929), 68.

Painting

Two words, above all others, describe the disposition of the artist, "inspiration" and "enthusiasm," and both have telling roots. "Enthusiasm" is derived from the Greek meaning "possession by the spirit." Needless to say, the world's greatest artists displayed each of these traits in abundance. The word "culture" is itself derived from the Latin "cultus" meaning worship, and the culture that begot Leonardo da Vinci and Michelangelo needs no introduction. According to one of his biographers, Michelangelo's works were "a stirring call to righteousness" by a soul in "vehement protest against evil."[31]

As a leading patron of the arts, the Church undoubtedly influenced choice of composition. Nevertheless, there were influential princes, dukes, emperors, and kings whose taste was secular. There were times, too, when artists suited themselves. Toward the end of his life, Michelangelo completed two canvases for his own satisfaction and both depicted Christ crucified.

High on anyone's list of classical painters would be Jan Van Eyck. As the most renowned northern European master of his day (1395-1441), Van Eyck pioneered in the rendering of dramatic contrast between light and dark tones for which the Flemish school would one day be famous. But another of his hallmarks was a partiality for biblical themes. In this respect, he anticipated Rembrandt, another believer who, in spite of the irregularity of his marital arrangements, was anything but a libertine.

Rembrandt was the only leader among Dutch painters of his time to devote himself primarily to religious themes. His earliest signed painting is that of the stoning of St. Stephen, and his favorite subjects thereafter were the flight of the Holy Family into Egypt (nine canvases), the Presentation by Mary of her son in the temple (another nine), and the Old Testament story of Tobias (fifty-five drawings, etchings, and paintings).

Shifting to the United States and leapfrogging several centuries, the most representative group of American artists, the Hudson

---

[31] See, for example, Symonds biography, 508, and Hurl biography, vi.

River School, could not have been more candid about its purpose, which was to focus on nature as a reflection of the Deity. Its founder, Thomas Cole, avowedly religious, feared the effects of materialism and idealized the Middle Ages for its knightly code of chivalry. Then, too, when America's most accomplished twentieth-century illustrator, Norman Rockwell, depicted a woman and her grandson giving thanks to the Almighty in a railway café with streetwise derelicts looking on at a respectful distance, it became his most popular work.

One of Rockwell's celebrated "Four Freedoms" shows people at prayer with hearts uplifted and, in the hands of a wrinkled old lady in the foreground, a rosary. "Lift Up Thine Eyes," another favorite, features pedestrians passing before the portal of a beautiful Gothic cathedral with eyes firmly fixed on the slate-gray sidewalk. Still another of his works, "Father and Son," presents two generations huddled together in a church pew preparing a passage to be read aloud. Although most of his subjects were necessarily secular to satisfy the taste of a secular patron, *The Saturday Evening Post*, many of his most successful works testify, in one way or another, to the importance of divine worship. Rockwell's most cherished day of the year was Christmas, and his last painting, left unfinished on the easel, depicts a Christian missionary instructing an Indian chief.

Architecture

In the field of architecture, nothing has ever surpassed the medieval cathedrals for sheer power of form and delicacy of detail except perhaps the Parthenon, a temple dedicated to Athena, virgin goddess of the Greeks. India's Taj Mahal reflects an equally strong belief in the hereafter. Built by a Mogul emperor of exceptionally fine character as a tribute to a beloved wife who died giving birth to their fourteenth child (she was his only wife and he had no concubines), it is covered with verses from the Koran. Then there is Paris' Sainte Chapelle, arguably the most dazzling exhibition of stained glass anywhere in the world, commissioned by Louis IX, a man of towering piety and social awareness. Bernini, the greatest architect and sculptor of the Italian baroque period, delighted in the spiritual exercises of St. Ignatius, while farther to the west, the exquisite Mexican temple pyramid at Chichen Itza, built at the high tide of devotion to the gods, affords yet another example of the result of religious enthusiasm. Subsequently, as faith in the supernatural began to wane, so too did Mayan art.

Censorship

From the perspective of not a few, religion means censorship. Yet what happens when God is removed from the picture? From 1917 until well into the 1980s, there was but one patron of the arts in Soviet Russia, an atheistic state. And the result? Censorship of such severity that the better artists were forced underground. From a broader perspective, it may be seen that the least religious century since the Dark Ages has produced, in addition to more stringent forms of censorship, painting, music, and literature commensurate with its spiritual aridity. There are exceptions, of course. But this, in the main, is what one finds.

And what of earlier epochs? Augustus, father of Rome's golden age, revived the office of censor, and similar constraints were imposed by Elizabeth I at the time of Shakespeare and Ben Jonson. Verdi's opera, *Rigoletto*, and Mozart's *Don Giovanni* were composed with an eye to the censors, and both enjoyed enormous success. French theater waxed brilliant under the heavy hand of the Sun King, Louis XIV, while Brazilian theater matured under a military dictatorship.

In a word, traditional forms of censorship seem to have brought out the best in artists, requiring of them that they rely less on sex, violence, and politics, and more on universal themes of enduring interest handled with skill and artistry. Americans lived happily for 175 years with censorship enshrined in countless statutes and city ordinances. In 1930, Hollywood adopted an Official Production Code written by a Jesuit priest and a Catholic layman. Four years later, the American bishops established the National Legion of Decency with film ratings of A-1, A-2, B, and C (Condemned). The heads of the movie studios responded by appointing a Catholic, Joseph Breen, to head the Production Code Administration; and for three decades, this was how things stood. It was the age of *Gone With the Wind*, *It's A Wonderful Life*, and *Casablanca*.[32]

The fact is that no one has ever been able to explain what is wrong with setting limits to what may be displayed in the name of art, for without limits, man runs amuck. Professor Himmelfarb, in her *De-Moralization of Society* (1995), observes that,

> In 1968, the English playwright and member of Parliament, A.P. Herbert had the satisfaction of witnessing the passage of the act he had sponsored abolishing censorship on stage. Only two years later, he complained that what had started as a "worthy struggle for reasonable liberty for honest writers" had ended as the "right to represent copulation, veraciously on the public stage." About the same time, a leading American civil liberties lawyer, Morris Ernst, was moved to protest that he had meant to ensure the publication of Joyce's *Ulysses*, "not the public performance of sodomy." (p. 249)

Science

Even in the world of science, where the goal is to unlock secrets of an already existing creation, there is plenty to suggest a positive relationship between God and man. The origins of modern science, which date from the late Middle Ages, are to be found not among the more secular Averroists of Padua but rather with the disciples of Roger Bacon and William Ockham, who viewed knowledge and religion as inextricably linked.

Three of the world's pioneer scientists were priests: Roger Bacon, Albert the Great, and Gregor Mendel. Among laymen, Prince Henry the Navigator, who paved the way for Vasco da Gama, thought of himself as an agent of evangelization. And one can add to the list Leonardo, Descartes, Newton, and Leibnitz —

---

[32] See Frank Walsh, *Sin and Censorship: The Catholic Church and the Motion Picture Industry*.

all men of faith, especially Newton, the most illustrious mathematician, astronomer, and physicist who ever lived. His theory of light, along with his laws of gravitation and motion, indeed his whole notion of how the universe is held together, served as the guiding principles of physics for three hundred years. They are still important. And this was an individual who filled his library with books on theology.

In our own day, the laser beam was invented by a man who found time to instruct young people in religion, Nobel Prize winner Dr. Charles Townes. There is also Michael Faraday, the dean of experimental scientists, who thought of his work as essentially a search for God. Galvani and Volta, whose names are associated with galvanized iron and electric voltage, were staunch Catholics, as was Louis Pasteur, father of pasteurization and inoculation. Madame Curie, Nobel Prize winner for her work in radioactivity and the discovery of radium, Guglielmo Marconi, inventor of the radio, Ampère in electricity, Laennec, inventor of the stethoscope, Lapparent in geology, and Dwight, the anatomist, were Catholic as well; similarly Fallopio, Laplace, and Magellan.

Nor are we yet finished. Robert Millikan, a noted American physicist, and Sir Arthur Stanley Eddington, another outstanding man of science, were cited by *Time* magazine for their religiosity. Leo Szilard, known by many during his lifetime as "the Jules Verne of Science," was a believer, too, as was Albert Einstein, who remarked that "science without religion is lame." For Einstein, reared in a Jewish home and educated at a Catholic parochial school, God was the source of all creativity.[33]

John Glenn, the first American to circle the earth in a spaceship, gave a talk entitled, "Why I know There Is A God" in which he marvelled at "the orderliness of the entire universe from the smallest atomic structure to the greatest thing we can visualize: galaxies millions of light years across, all traveling in exact prescribed orbits in relation to one another."

It would be difficult, if not impossible, to say how many other names in the constellation of scientific genius were God-fearing,

---

[33] "The more I study science," remarked Einstein, "the more I believe in God" (*Wall Street Journal*, December 24, 1997, p. A10).

but among them is Bernard Riemann, one of the most important mathematicians and theoretical physicists of the nineteenth century. Alongside Riemann stands Admiral Hyman Rickover, known to Americans as the father of the atomic submarine. "Oh God," mused Rickover, "Thy sea is so great, and my ship so small!" There is Lord Kelvin, British mathematician, physicist, and inventor, who believed himself "forced by science" to embrace religion. Wernher von Braun, who ran the United States rocket program during the 1960s and designed the Jupiter C rocket which lifted the first American earth satellite into space, was another man of faith. Finally, we must not forget the first men to circle the moon: James A. Lovell, Jr., Frank Borman, and William Anders. All three were regular churchgoers, while Eugene Cernan, first of the astronauts to walk completely around planet earth, was a daily communicant.[34]

It is interesting to note that scientific discoveries of the twentieth century have pretty well neutralized the appeal of secular theories advanced during the late 1800s. The "Big Bang" theory currently favored by cosmologists to explain the origin of the universe squares nicely with Genesis' "Let there be light!" From the latest research, we also know that if gravity were any more powerful than it is (or any less powerful), human life would never have been possible. Furthermore, in the light of quantum physics, matter is beginning to assume almost magical qualities — more akin to a thought than a machine — and the question is: whose thought?[35]

Government

In politics it is the exception that proves the rule. Government officials are not normally known for their piety. But those with the

---

[34] For the material on science and religion, I am much indebted to Scott, *Space Age Scientists* (1970).

[35] *Wall Street Journal*, December 24, 1997, p. A10. One might add that Norbert Wiener, father of cybernetics, held that "science is impossible without faith"; and Jerome Lejeune, who discovered the chromosome disorder that leads to Down's syndrome, is a leader in the French Catholic Pro-Life Movement.

most spectacular record of achievement, among them Ramses II (the Great) of Egypt, Octavian (Caesar Augustus), Charlemagne, Alfred the Great of England, Louis IX of France, Otto the Great of Germany, Isabella of Spain, and Maria Theresa of Austria, were deeply committed to religious observance.

In America, William Henry Harrison, Zachary Taylor, Millard Fillmore, Ulysses Grant, Chester Arthur, William Howard Taft, and Warren Gamaliel Harding, among the least religious of presidents, are also among the least great. Conversely, all of the greats, virtually without exception, were vocally religious.[36] George Washington attended church services weekly, supported a state-sponsored religious establishment in his native Virginia, and formulated the addition to the presidential oath, "So help me God."[37] The first four presidents all proclaimed national days of fasting, and Thomas Jefferson, son of a church warden, supported a Virginia bill in 1735 to punish "Sabbath breakers." Jefferson may have been a Deist, but like his democratic confreres, he believed religion necessary for a healthy republic.

The Founding Fathers are an instructive lot. John Jay, first chief justice of the Supreme Court, headed the American Bible Society. James Madison, father of the Constitution, echoed Washington and Jefferson in proclaiming God "essential to the moral order of the world and the happiness of man." And John Adams, second president and father of another chief executive, held that the notion of equality upon which America was built presupposed a God. This, in turn, shaped his view of what children should be taught: "Let them revere nothing but religion, morality, and liberty."

Adams' cousin, Samuel, as delegate from Massachusetts to the Continental Congress, pressed for public prayer. And a few years later, Benjamin Franklin proposed that each session of the Constitutional Convention open with an invocation to the Almighty (fifty-two out of fifty-five delegates were practicing Christians). Inventor

---

[36] See Edmund Fuller and David Green's volume on the religious views of the presidents.

[37] See R. Hughes, *George Washington*, III, 282-83, and Stephen Carter, *The Culture of Disbelief*, 99-100.

of the lightening rod and sophisticate par excellence, Franklin nonetheless regarded the Bible as "the most faithful of all histories."[38]

It is doubtful that there has ever been a more avid reader of scripture than Abraham Lincoln, another son of a church warden. "I can see how it might be possible for a man to look down into the mud and be an atheist," he once said, "but I cannot conceive how he could look up into the heavens and say there is no God."[39]

Closer to our own time, big-game hunter and Nobel Prize winner Theodore Roosevelt advocated regular churchgoing, while Woodrow Wilson announced a national day of prayer for the deliverance of Europe during World War II and declared, "I believe in Divine Providence."[40]

In light of the foregoing, it should come as no surprise to find leading statesmen of the post-World War II generation more religious as a group than the age in which they lived. This is particularly true of Adenauer, de Gaulle, de Gasperi of Italy, and John Foster Dulles.[41] Dwight D. Eisenhower and Ronald Reagan, two presidents with impressive records at home and abroad, may be cited as well, since they were far from indifferent when it came to religion. Reagan's rhetoric and memoirs are positively peppered with references to God, and Ike, who grew up in a deeply spiritual atmosphere, remarked on one occasion that "recognition" of a "Supreme Being" is the "first and most basic expression of Americanism."[42]

---

[38] For Franklin's religious sentiment and belief in divine providence, see his "Address to the United States of America" published in *Gentlemen's Magazine* (London), February, 1789, vol. 59, pt. 1. For the Madison quote, see William McNeil Burns, *The American Idea of Mission*, chapter 8. For the lines from Adams, see *William and Mary Quarterly*, Series 3, #7, p. 244. See also Phyllis Lee Levin's biography of Abigail Adams, 44, 54-55. One of the best works on religion and the Founding Fathers is by Benjamin Hart: *Faith and Freedom* (1988), especially the last two chapters, as long as one is willing to discount his uninformed criticism of Catholicism.

[39] Herndon, *Lincoln*, I, 41.

[40] From a speech given at San Francisco (Wilson quote).

[41] On Eisenhower and Dulles, see Frederick W. Marks, *Power and Peace: The Diplomacy of John Foster Dulles*, 4, 24-25, 119-25.

[42] Carter, *Culture*, 100. God is mentioned six times in the first fifty-seven pages of Reagan's autobiography, *An American Life*, as well as on pages 70, 123, 168, 226, 263, 322, 399, 402, 455, and 475.

Chapter 2

The Case for Christ

Having established in Chapter I that belief in God makes sense, that it is physically, as well as morally, beneficial, and having argued further that it makes men happy and opens the sluice gates of creativity, we may now turn our attention to the claims of one religion in particular.

The case for Christianity hinges on a series of questions. Who can deny that the world's calendar is fixed on the fulcrum of a single birth — the birth, moreover, of a man who never took an advanced degree, never wrote a book, and never held public office? Jesus never traveled more than three hundred miles from his native village, never owned a home or did any of the things normally associated with greatness. Yet he has exerted more influence over mankind than all of the kings and emperors who ever lived. How, one is moved to inquire, did a small splinter group of Jews without intellectual or social distinction, a company of outcasts scorned and rejected by Roman, Greek, and Jew alike, wrest control of the Roman Empire and spread its faith almost overnight to Ethiopia, Ukraine, and India?

How can one read the gospels of Matthew, Mark, Luke, and John without marveling at their singular beauty and originality, without being struck by the force of their logic, and without wondering if the events that they relate, nothing less than the greatest story ever told, could be the work of mere men?

How, thirdly, account for the fact that Jesus' blistering denunciation of the religious establishment of his day, coupled with a warning of impending doom, was followed within forty years of his death by the most catastrophic event of all time for the Jewish people: destruction of their temple and, along with it, the genealogical records upon which their priesthood was based. To this day, Judaism has neither priests nor sacrifice. Hundreds of thousands of Jews perished at the hands of Titus' soldiers in 70 A.D., and by the end of Hadrian's reign (183 A.D.), the remainder of the Jewish populace, with few exceptions, was scattered and sold into slavery.

Jesus predicted this debacle, observing that his brethren "knew not the hour of their visitation" nor what was "for their peace" (Lk. 19:41-44) and warning too of the peril of excessive nationalism. He had tried to dispel bitterness against the Roman occupation. He had wept over the fate of Jerusalem. But to no avail. Insurrection and guerrilla warfare on the part of the Jews proceeded apace until Rome opted for a radical solution.

Surely, one of the most trenchant arguments for the existence of God is Jesus himself, for here was one who not only spoke confidently of God but claimed to *be* God and proved it by working miracles — more of them, and on a grander scale, than anyone before or since. He cured leprosy and blindness. He changed water into wine. He fed thousands with a handful of loaves. His apostles watched as he walked on water and restored a severed ear to the head of its owner. Both Elijah and Elisha raised a person from the dead, but Jesus raised several. Needless to say, his own resurrection, which he foretold on several occasions, constitutes his greatest claim to divinity.[43] Neither Mohammed nor Buddha, neither Zoroaster nor Confucius — nor any other sage, for that matter — can come even on this score. No one else condemned whole towns and classes of people or wound up on a cross for what he had to say — voluntarily. Jesus freely surrendered himself into the hands of sworn enemies out of a sense of duty commingled with love.

His followers, as we shall see, gave their lives in incredible numbers as a witness to his resurrection. And all of this during a period when eyewitnesses proliferated.

---

[43] See, for example, Mk. 8:31.

Prophet Extraordinary

Jesus was no ordinary preacher. Where others called for repentance, he spoke authoritatively of the consequences of virtue and vice: heaven and hell. He described poverty and celibacy as divine gifts. Restoring marriage to its original state, he ruled out polygamy and divorce. His insistence on love of enemies and the fusing of every tribe and nation into a people of one faith are as fresh today as they were then. What other Jewish leader ever made a role model of Roman soldiers and Samaritans (Mt. 8:10; Lk. 10:33)?

Here was a teacher who could be blindingly direct and uncompromising: "Be ye perfect," he insisted, "even as your heavenly Father is perfect" (Mt. 5:48). His celebrated Sermon on the Mount is no vague testimonial to peacemakers and the poor but rather a catalogue of thirty-one highly specific moral admonitions, fifteen of them in the form of "don'ts." He preached purity and self-effacement. He founded a Church to shepherd his flock until the end of time, telling Peter, "I give you the keys to the kingdom of heaven, and whatever you bind on earth shall be bound in heaven" (Mt. 16:18-19). And later: "Whose sins you forgive, they are forgiven (John 20:23)...." "Go therefore and make disciples of all nations, baptizing them [and] ... teaching them to observe all that I have commanded you (Mt.28:19-20)...." "He who hears you hears me" (Lk.10:16).

Mary's son declared himself wiser than Solomon and greater as a minister of the word than Jonah (Mt.12:41-42). Necessarily reticent about the supernatural side of his makeup because anything else would have been regarded as blasphemous under the Mosaic law and punishable by death, he employed subtlety in registering claims to divinity, especially at the outset of his public life. So, too, when spelling out his revolutionary moral code, did he speak in the form of parables so as to distance himself from unreceptive listeners, a divinely courteous tactic.

But however muted and indirect Jesus' claims, they were astonishing. Presenting himself as sinless (John 8:46), he undertook to forgive the sins of his followers (Lk.5:20). He welcomed the title "Lord": "You call me master and Lord and you say well for so I am" (John 13:13), and on a number of occasions his disciples are described as having literally worshiped him (e.g. Mt.14:33; 20:20; 28:9; John 9:38).

"Before Abraham came to be," he said, "I am" (John 8:58) and "He who has seen me has seen the Father" (John 14:9). Laying claim to kinship with God "before the world existed" (John 17:5, 24) and to possession of all "that belongs to the Father" (John 16:15), he styled himself "Lord of the Sabbath" (Lk. 6:5). And, as if this were not enough, he insisted on *being* the truth: "I am the way, the truth, and the life" (John 14:6).

Some have held that the author of these words was simply a great religious leader, extraordinarily close to God, but not God himself. Yet how could this be? Jewish spokesmen, after examining him, were crystal clear on the meaning of his message: "Thou, a man, makest thyself God" (John 10:31-33). One of two conclusions appears inescapable: either Jesus was the person he claimed to be on numerous occasions and in numerous ways — namely God — or he was a colossal egotist and fraud. But what fraud ever spoke as he spoke or taught as he taught? To his foes he was, and remains, an enigma.

Although it has been suggested that he may have suffered from mental illness, this makes little sense in clinical terms as the "divinity complex" is a recognized form of psychopathology characterized by inflexibility, dullness, and predictability. Jesus was at all times creative, interesting, and unpredictable.[44]

He is the only leader, moreover, whose coming has ever been foretold. Old Testament predictions range from a virginal conception to birth in Bethlehem and the undergoing of torture and humiliation for the sins of mankind. Taken individually, the prophecies are striking; considered in their entirety they are stupefying. Christian interpretation of the Messianic texts may be open to question. But down to the present day, Jewish commentators have been at a loss to offer any convincing alternative.[45]

---

[44] Kreeft and Tacelli, *Handbook of Christian Apologetics* (1994), 159.

[45] Jesus is the only religious leader whose coming was clearly foretold. An expert on Jewish history and culture has estimated that the rabbis at the time of Christ's birth had identified 456 passages in the Old Testament that described the coming of the long-awaited Messiah. The chance that one messianic prophecy would be fulfilled in Christ – for example, the prediction that

While the exact dates of Jesus' birth and death are unknown (circa 6 B.C. to 30 A.D.), there are references to him and his associates in contemporary accounts, both Jewish and Gentile. Tacitus, the greatest of all Roman historians and a stickler for accuracy, speaks of his execution under Pontius Pilate while Suetonius mentions him briefly in his biography of Claudius.

[45 cont.] He would be a direct descendant in the male line of King David – is perhaps one in a hundred. Abraham Lincoln had four children; yet there are no male descendants of Lincoln alive today that bear the family name. The chance that two prophecies would be fulfilled in Christ is perhaps one in a thousand. Let us add, for the sake of argument, the prophecy that the promised Messiah would be born in the small town of Bethlehem. The chance that anyone would fulfill all the prophecies, as Our Lord did, has been estimated as 1 in 84,000,000,000,000,000,000,000,000,000. Actually, this number requires two additional zeros.

The interpretation of prophetic texts is far from easy. But some of the more striking examples of Old Testament prophecy that find fulfillment in Jesus are as follows:

Psalm 22, which begins, "My God, My God, why have you forsaken me?" In verses 8-10 and 17-19, we read, "all who see me scoff at me; they mock me ... a pack of evildoers closes in upon me; they have pierced my hands and my feet; they look on and gloat over me; they divide my garments among them, and for my vesture they cast lots."

Isaiah 7:13-14: "Listen, O house of David!... The Lord himself will give you this sign: the virgin shall be with child and bear a son...."

Isaiah 49:6: "It is too little ... for you to be my servant, to raise up the tribes of Jacob, and restore the survivors of Israel; I will make you a light to the Gentiles, that my salvation may reach to the ends of the earth."

Isaiah 53, which describes God's suffering servant: he is spurned by men, a man of suffering (verse 3); he is "pierced for our offenses, crushed for our sins" (verse 5); "a grave" is assigned him "among the wicked" (verse 9).

Micah 5:1-4, which says, "But you, Bethlehem ... from you shall come forth for me one who is to be ruler in Israel.... His greatness shall reach to the ends of the earth."

Zechariah 9:9, which says, "See, your king shall come to you; a just savior is he, meek and riding on an ass."

It may be of interest to note two other Old Testament prophecies that have been fulfilled. The cities of Tyre and Babylon were, at the time of the prophesies, as great and commercially important as Chicago and New York are today. The prediction was that both would be utterly destroyed, and within a relatively short space of time, both were indeed destroyed. Babylon was soon nothing but a Persian game park and Tyre a simple fishing village. See Isaiah 13:19-21 and Ezekiel 26:12-14.

Phlegon, the freedman of Hadrian, records an eclipse of the sun at the death of Jesus, and Josephus, the leading Jewish historian of his time, born at Jerusalem in 37 A.D., records Christ's death under Pilate and his appearance on the third day (Sunday) to a group of disciples.[46] There are Roman inscriptions as well indicating that he was crucified under Pontius Pilate.[47] Mary and her son are even mentioned in early versions of the Talmud which, to Jews, is second in prestige only to the Bible.

The Resurrection

Jewish writings do not deny any of the sayings or actions attributed to Jesus save one, his resurrection. As late as the fourth and fifth centuries, when Christian apologists asked Jewish authorities if they had any basis for denying Christ's miracles, the answer was silence.[48] The rabbis had little to lose and everything to gain from blanket denials had they felt their people would take them seriously. But such disclaimers were not forthcoming. While they stoned Stephen, executed James, and drove the Christian community out of Jerusalem, they accepted Jesus' miracles implicitly, charging only that he used sorcery or appeals to the devil.

Why, then, did they reject the Resurrection? We know where the remains of Abraham, Mohammed, Buddha, and Confucius are buried. But Jesus' tomb is empty. Naturally, when the chief priests found they could not produce his corpse, they were embarrassed. And so they spread rumors that some disciples came and stole the body from the tomb. Such a charge cannot be permitted to stand, for, as St. Paul points out in his first letter to the Corinthians, our faith is in vain if Christ did not rise from the dead (15:14).

The first point worthy of notice in this connection is that gospel descriptions of miraculous happenings at the moment of Jesus'

---

[46]   The authenticity of this passage is disputed by the Jews as they have no record of Josephus ever having converted.

[47]   See, for example, Tacitus' *Annals* (Book 15). One may turn to Suetonius, who was Roman, as well as to the patrician Jew, Josephus. See also, in this connection, *Catholic Digest*, October, 1994, p. 100.

[48]   Hilarin Felder, *Christ and the Critics* (1924), II, 294-95.

death — tombs of the prophets being opened and the veil of the temple being rent from top to bottom — are paralleled by Talmudic accounts of a mysterious opening of the massive brass gate of the inner temple in the year 30 A.D. So heavy was the gate that as many as twenty men were required to open it, and Josephus confirms a rent in the curtain.[49]

Secondly, it is hard to deny the authenticity of the gospel narratives when "an immense multitude" of Christians, to quote Tacitus, chose a painful death over denial of the contents of these very narratives within thirty years of the crucifixion.[50] Some were thrown to the lions. Others were doused with oil and set aflame as human torches to light the way to the arena for evening games. Men and women died in unspeakable torment.

Why, thirdly, would Christian leaders circulate fraudulent accounts when such material placed their very lives in jeopardy and they could be contradicted by an army of eyewitnesses?

Could the Resurrection have been a product of hallucination? Five hundred at a time saw the risen Christ, according to Paul (1 Cor. 15:6), and ghosts do not eat, as the resurrected Lord did. Neither can one accuse the disciples of credulity when they refused to believe until they could see with their own eyes. Then, too, hallucinations last only a few seconds or minutes, and normally they occur only once. Jesus is recorded as having appeared many times to many people for lengthy intervals.

Could it be that Jesus merely slipped into a coma on the cross as a prelude to making good his escape from the tomb? Again, the evidence suggests otherwise. Procedures of crucifixion under Roman law were expressly designed to guard against such a possibility; indeed soldiers were liable to execution for allowing a capital prisoner to go free. That Jesus' legs were not broken, as were those of his companions on the cross, can only mean that his executioners were certain of his death. Nevertheless, as an added precaution, they pierced his side with a lance. Blood and water were observed flowing from the wound, indicating that his lungs had collapsed and he had died from asphyxiation.

---

[49]   Warren Carroll, *The Founding of Christendom*, 374-75, 391-92.
[50]   Dostoyevsky and Kierkegaard, along with others, thought not.

How, furthermore, could anyone undergo a severe beating, lose blood from his temples, wrists, feet and side, forego food and water for days and yet muster enough strength to remove a huge stone from the entrance to his tomb under the eyes of an elite guard?

According to Jewish leaders, the sentries fell asleep, and Jesus' disciples spirited his body away in the night. How likely is it, though, that all members of the guard would have fallen asleep at the same time given the fact that their livelihood, not to say their lives, required the utmost vigilance?

Further questions arise. Why would the disciples put their lives on the line to recover a corpse? Where would they store it? How long would such heroics remain secret? How likely is it that body snatchers would have taken the time to remove Jesus' burial cloths and fold the handkerchief which had covered his head, as recounted by John (20:6-8)? How likely, in addition, that the apostles, even the boldest among them, would have had the nerve and the stamina to pull off a coup of this magnitude when Christian morale had been completely shattered?

It has been well said that if the story of Jesus' victory over death is false, then Matthew, Mark, Luke, and John were the cleverest fantasists who ever lived, far surpassing Dante, Shakespeare, and Tolkien.[51]

The Case for Scripture

The final refuge of skeptics is denial of the authenticity of scripture. Fortunately, Christ's resurrection does not depend on the gospels. It figures in the letters of Barnabus, Clement, Polycarp, and Ignatius of Antioch. Some time later, Irenaeus tells of having heard Polycarp, a student of John, describe Jesus' miracles.[52]

But even if the gospels were all one had to go on, there would still be scant room for doubt. No reputable scholar believes that the synoptic gospels (Matthew, Mark, and Luke) were written later than 80-90 A.D., and current estimates tend to be on the side

---

[51] Kreeft and Tacelli, *Handbook*, 185.
[52] For material on the Resurrection, I am indebted to Hayes, Hayes, and Drummey, *Christianity and Reason*, an excellent resource.

of an earlier date. This means that many people who heard Jesus preach, saw him work cures, and witnessed his death were alive when the gospels were written and thus in a position to set the record straight. Quadratus, an early apologist, tells us there were persons abroad as late as 123 A.D. who had been cured by Jesus or raised from the dead.

Those who hold that the original accounts were tampered with must reckon with the fact that Paul's letters, written within the lifetime of eyewitnesses to Christ's miracles, affirm all the major claims of the four evangelists; also that the earliest of the Church Fathers quote scripture in its present form. Clement of Rome (d. 98 A.D.), for example, quotes the gospel of John (7:13); Ignatius of Antioch (d. 107) quotes extensively from Matthew, as well as John; and Matthew, Mark, and John find an echo in Papias (circa 60-135 A.D.), as well as in Polycarp.

Extant sources are especially impressive considering that leaders of the early church were discriminating. They accepted certain writings and rejected others. Among the discarded texts are the proto-gospel of James, the Arabic Gospel of the Childhood of Christ, various gospels of the Hebrews and Egyptians, and the gospels of the Ebionites.[53] In only one instance is a spurious or apocryphal gospel ever quoted by an identifiable author during the first three hundred years after Christ.

There is a third reason for ruling out the possibility of tampering. Quotes and references similar to those mentioned above are contained in the *Didache*, an important and widely circulated compendium of Christian teaching and practice dated between 60 and 90 A.D.

Fourthly, considering that the Church spread so rapidly over such great distances carrying the written and spoken word wherever it went, it is fair to assume that false editing in one place would have been exposed by comparison with texts circulating elsewhere. In 110 A.D., the dissident Marcion fabricated a gospel specially tailored to suit his brand of heresy, and it triggered universal protest.

A fifth argument for authenticity stems from the number and type of early Church manuscripts in our possession. By comparison

---

[53] Doornik, Jelsma, and Lisdonk, *Handbook of the Catholic Faith* (1956), 76.

with only two copies of Tacitus, there are thousands of gospel texts in good condition that contain part or all of the gospel, as we know it today, and they date from the second century onward, including one from the third century that transcribes a complete gospel.

The fact that early manuscript copies of the gospels, which are available in many languages, are dated in such close proximity to the era of eyewitnesses is quite extraordinary. The next most reliable classical manuscript after the gospels is a copy of Homer's *Iliad*, which is dated 500 years from the time of composition. With Caesar's *Commentaries*, the gap is 900 years, with Herodotus 1,000.

Furthermore, out of thousands of manuscript copies that have survived, either in whole or in part, from the second and third century onward, only a few hundred contain changes in wording that could have any appreciable impact on meaning. Of these, a mere fifteen touch on anything historical or dogmatic. And none of the fifteen casts the slightest doubt on any element of Christian dogma.[54] Tampering with the originals, unless all were altered in precisely the same way, would almost surely have produced textual discrepancies of a more substantive kind. The latest discoveries of ancient texts such as the Dead Sea Scrolls serve only to confirm the historicity and reliability of the New Testament.

As the Oxford-trained historian and convert to Catholicism Christopher Dawson once put it, "We possess fuller and more authentic documents on the birth of Christianity than that of any other world religion."[55]

Naysayers must reckon with innumerable place-names, dates, and statistics ranging from the size of crowds and weather conditions to official titles, idioms, methods of travel, and peculiarities of place, that no one in the second century, however well read, even if they had been Jewish, could possibly have duplicated. One finds homely details perched alongside the loftiest philosophical passages. Would a scheming author tell us, without any further explanation, that at the time of Our Lord's arrest, an unnamed man fled away naked into the night (Mk. 14:52)? Would a duplicitous gospel writer

---

[54] Ibid., 80. See also Metzger, *The Text of the New Testament: Its Transmission, Corruption, and Restoration* (1993).

[55] Christopher Dawson, *Christianity and the New Age* (1985 reprint), 69.

take the trouble to report that Jesus charged an audience to "tell no one" about one of his miracles (Mk. 7:36)? Would he name women as the first witnesses of the Resurrection when male testimony was the only kind admissible in Jewish courts of law?

Why so many apparent inconsistencies, some of them embarrassing to the Christian cause, if the gospel narratives were the work of cunning opportunists? Would charlatans record Jesus' words on the cross, "My God, my God, why have you forsaken me?" (Mt. 27:46) when Our Savior claimed to *be* God and was presented as such by his followers? Would Matthew quote Jesus in one instance as saying, "Let your works shine before men" and in another as cautioning, "Take heed not to do your good before men in order to be seen by them" (5:16 vs. 6:1)? Christ is quoted by turns as having taught that "Few will enter [the kingdom of heaven]," and at the same time, "Many will come from the east and from the west and will feast with Abraham and Isaac and Jacob" (Mt. 7:13-14 vs. 8:11-12). Not that there are any instances of apparent contradiction or inconsistency that cannot be resolved. But why would fakers want to tax the mind of the average reader? Why, above all, are there four different and differing gospel accounts? Why not one?

Whether or not all four gospels were written by the authors whose names are attached to them remains a moot question. However, there is impressive testimony on the side of tradition: the Epistle of Barnabas, the Epistle of Clement, and the Shepherd of Hermas, for example. One can cite, in addition, the opinion of Theophilus, Hippolytus, Origen, Quadratus, Irenaeus, Melito, Polycarp, Justin Martyr, Dionysius, Tertullian, Cyprian, Tatian, Caius, Athanasius, and Cyril. Papias, a first century disciple of John the Apostle, wrote that one named Matthew first wrote in Hebrew and that one named Mark wrote what he had heard from Peter. The Muratorian Fragment, dating from 170 A.D. at the latest, tells us that the third gospel was written by Luke and the fourth by John. Even such outspoken opponents of the faith as Celsus, Porphyry, and Emperor Julian conceded the Church's position on authorship.[56]

---

[56] Kreeft and Tacelli, *Handbook*, 194; Rumble and Carty, *Radio Replies*, I, 23-24.

Beyond this, there is compelling internal evidence. Luke, for example, is said to have been a physician, and this is borne out by his choice of words. The term he uses for needle signifies a surgical needle, just as he alone, among the four evangelists, recalls that Jesus sweated blood in the Garden of Gethsemane. Matthew, who is thought to have been a tax collector, makes frequent reference to coins and money. He is also the only writer who recounts Christ's payment of the temple tax (Mt. 17:23-26). There is no dearth of examples.

For those who doubt that Matthew, Mark, Luke, and John could recall Jesus' words fifteen, twenty, or fifty years after the event with any degree of accuracy, the answer is twofold. First, Our Lord promised a special form of divine inspiration when he said he would send the Holy Spirit to "bring to your mind whatever I have said to you" (John 14:26). Secondly, the people of Jesus' time excelled in feats of memory. Reading and writing were not generally taught owing to the scarcity and high cost of materials. Consequently, knowledge had to be transmitted orally in ways designed to aid retention. Rhymes, rhythms, and "ABCDalian" (each line beginning with a successive letter of the alphabet) were among the techniques employed. Repetition, another method, is found in the Beatitudes: "Blessed are the poor ... Blessed are ... Blessed are ..." The rabbis used to say that a good student, like a good cistern, never leaked.

As recently as the early 1800s, in the hallowed halls of the United States Senate, orators of the stature of Webster, Clay, and Calhoun were known to hold forth by the hour without benefit of notes owing to their boyhood training. As students they performed in a way we would regard today as well-nigh impossible. According to Calhoun's biographer, he attended an academy where the weaker students were expected to memorize dozens of lines a day.[57]

History is overwhelmingly on the side of scripture. There was a time when scholars questioned gospel accounts of cures at the pool of Bethesda. Pentagonal shapes were not thought to have existed in Palestinian architecture until a later date, and Bethesda is described as having five porticoes. Recent excavations tell a different story: namely, that pentagonal shapes predated the gospel.

---

[57] Margaret Coit, *John C. Calhoun* (paperback), 15.

Lot's testimony regarding the fertility of the lower Jordan Valley, long in doubt, has also been vindicated.

Or take the apostles' surprise at Jesus' prediction that the Jewish temple would be physically destroyed. There seemed no logical basis for their wonderment until a 600-ton stone was discovered among its ruins. Here was a structure built to last. Then there was Herod's slaughter of the Innocents. Could a man whose rule lasted so long have behaved so reprehensibly? The answer lies in Jewish records. Herod murdered his wife, his mother and his children, along with members of the Sanhedrin.[58]

Occasionally, one comes across a discrepancy between Holy Writ and the secular record. It is well to remember at such times that pagan clerks were not infallible. Moreover, the sacred writers themselves may have been approximating dates or events. In today's parlance, a phrase like "back in the days of George Washington" can be interpreted as referring to an entire era embracing years which predate and postdate the actual period of Washington's life.[59]

Then, too, because the inspired writers may have written informally and according to appearance (much as we might say today that "the sun rose" or "the sun set"), allowances must be made for their intent. Was the Book of Jonah, for example, conceived as a strict chronicle of events or as a story meant to edify and instruct? For some, Jonah's three-day incarceration in the belly of a whale is pure myth. On the other hand, scientists have never denied the possibility of human survival under such circumstances. Wallechninsky and Wallace report that in February 1891, after the ship *Star of the East* landed an eighty-foot sperm whale, a missing seaman by the name of James Bartley was presumed drowned. But the next day, when the crew began carving up its catch, Bartley was found inside the stomach — alive.[60] Since no one has ever handed down an authoritative ruling on how literally the Book of Jonah is to be interpreted, there is room for speculation.

---

[58] See Rev. William G. Most, *Free From All Error: Authorship, Inerrancy, Historicity of Scripture, Church Teaching, and Modern Scripture Scholars* (1985, reprinted 1990).

[59] See the *Constitution on Divine Revelation*, n. 11; also Most, *Free From All Error*, 69-70 and 87-89.

[60] Most, *Free From All Error*, 58.

Some profess to be scandalized by a God who would instruct Joshua to obliterate the heathen tribes of Canaan.[61] But, as in the case of the flood, this was clearly a punishment for immorality.[62] Did God do wrong to rain fire and brimstone on Sodom and Gomorrah? Where is it written that the Sovereign Lord of the Universe is bound to act in accordance with human norms? "My thoughts are not your thoughts, nor are my ways your ways, says the Lord."[63] It is we who must measure up to God's standards rather than the other way around.

Withal, it is doubtful if any books in all of recorded history have been as closely scrutinized as Matthew, Mark, Luke, and John. Attacks and exposés have followed, one upon another, all reflecting the preoccupation or mind-set of a given age. And all of them, without exception, have boomeranged; for each time a novel objection gains currency, only to prove groundless, it begets a corresponding increase in confidence among orthodox scholars and exegetes.[64]

Christian Culture

By this time, the reader may be thinking that all the miracles in the world, backed by airtight arguments for the authenticity of scripture, will not vindicate a system of belief unless it can be shown that mankind is somehow better off for having embraced it. Granted, if Jesus was God, then we have a right to expect something out of the ordinary from the Church that he founded.

And what do we find? As early as the Roman imperial period, Christian authors were writing with a freshness and excitement notably absent in the work of their contemporaries.[65] Augustine, Jerome, Ambrose, and other members of the early Church posi-

---

61   Acts 13:19; Joshua 10:40; 11:14-15, 20. See also Joshua 8:7-8, 24-27; 10:12-13, 28-43.

62   Deut. 7:1-6; 20:16-18.

63   Isaiah 55:8.

64   Most's *Free From All Error* is excellent on inerrancy. See also Stewart Custer, *Does Inspiration Demand Inerrancy?* (1968) and F. F. Bruce, *The New Testament Documents* (1983). Custer is especially good on reconciliation of alleged inconsistency and contradiction (pp. 93-114).

65   McManners, ed., *Oxford Illustrated History*, 61.

tively dominated the intellectual world of their time. It was Christianity that introduced the ideal of general education based on the rationality of the universe. And by the end of the Middle Ages, at a time when the Buddhist Orient could boast only a handful of schools of any type, Christian England and Wales, with a population of about 2,500,000, supported approximately 400 grammar schools, a better ratio than obtained in Victorian times. It may also be pointed out, in line with the Christian emphasis on education, that Japanese and Chinese converts to the faith have made scientific discoveries over the years that are out of all proportion to their numbers and influence in Oriental society.[66]

Faith in the God-man affected disparate areas. Clerics championed the "just price" theory in merchandising and opposed the exploitation of foreigners. On one occasion, an outraged monk named Telemachus, seated among the spectators at a Roman gladiatorial contest in which competitors were obliged to fight to the death, leaped into the arena in a valiant attempt to stop the bloodshed. He fell beneath a flashing sword when occupants of the imperial box gave him "thumbs down." But it was the last such contest ever staged in Rome.

Other forms of cruelty, including crucifixion, were eliminated by Constantine and his successors under Christian prodding. Not until secular humanism reemerges during the Renaissance does one hear again of "Roman torture," unknown during the so-called "Dark Ages."[67] Along the same line, but somewhat later, at the Catholic Council of Trent (1545-63), dueling was outlawed, albeit unsuccessfully.

The same humanizing — or should one say "divinizing" — impact of Christianity is evident in its opposition to human sacrifice. Eighty thousand people were stabbed to death and their hearts torn out during priestly ceremonies marking the dedication of the Aztec temple of Huitzilopochtli in 1487.[68] Christianity put an end to this around the same time that it eradicated cannibalism in the Caribbean. Similarly, Christian revulsion at Chinese foot-binding

---

[66] *Encyclopaedia Britannica*, 14th ed., VII, 986b.
[67] William Thomas Walsh, *Isabella of Spain*, 179.
[68] Warren Carroll, *The Glory of Christendom* (1993), 576.

of female infants and ritual suicide by Indian widows was a factor in their eventual disappearance.

Other bonds of servitude were loosened. One restriction after another was placed on slaveholders following Rome's conversion to Christianity until slavery itself became virtually extinct. It made a comeback in the wake of the barbarian invasions. But the Church's stress on human dignity, coupled with its work on behalf of emancipation, prevailed.

Slavery erupted with renewed vigor in the fifteenth and sixteenth centuries, a period of rising nationalism and waning papal influence. But opponents imbued with the spirit of the gospel returned to the charge, especially during the late eighteenth and early nineteenth centuries. The history of other religions suggests that the abolitionist movement would have been greatly delayed, if not altogether missing, in anything but a Christian environment.[69] William Wilberforce, mainstay of the British antislavery crusade, headed the Evangelical Society of his country and presided over a household where religion clearly mattered. Three of his four sons converted to Catholicism.

The Place of Women

Christianity had no sooner gained ascendancy in Rome than the status of women, both as maidens and wives, began to change. Society venerated virginity in honor of Mary, and not a few among the laity chose celibacy in imitation of Jesus, John the Baptist, and St. Paul.

Woman could no longer be forced into marriage without their consent; and pagan husbands, long accustomed to sleep with domestic slavegirls, were expected to love their wives as they loved their own bodies (Eph 5:28). Infanticide disappeared, and family life flourished as never before under the Church's ban on divorce. Justin (c. 100-165) and other Church Fathers, following Paul's example, went so far as to discourage remarriage even in the case of widows.[70]

---

[69] Ibid., 575.
[70] McManners, ed., *Oxford Illustrated History*, 39.

All of this marked a profound change in social mores, for when Jesus walked the streets of Nazareth, Rome had divorce by consent; Athens boasted of its total disregard of marriage; Peking harbored appalling vice; and Jerusalem tolerated polygamy and divorce. Under the new dispensation, men and women were regarded as equal in the eyes of God. At the time of the Nativity, the birth of a Jewish male was cause for celebration. Musicians serenaded parents amid universal gladness and congratulation. But if the new arrival happened to be a girl, the musicians would depart regretfully and in silence.[71] Not so in Christian households.

Women also benefitted from a movement to honor the rights of non-combatants during the period 400-1200. Under the Truce of God, war was outlawed during certain days and periods of the year, while under the Peace of God, designated areas were declared safe havens. As time passed, the intervals of peace and areas of refuge grew more and more numerous. At the same time, respect for the weak, especially women and children, became commonplace under the code of medieval chivalry.

Increasingly, women were exempted from the draft, even as they continued to enlist in military campaigns on a voluntary basis. Joan of Arc (1412-31), commander-in-chief of the French armies, was not as much of an anomaly as one might suppose. Four centuries before Joan mounted her charger, Countess Matilda of Tuscany (1046-1115) ruled most of northern Italy and led troops into battle. Women fought in the Second Crusade (1144-88), and after Joan's time, they entered combat on the Protestant side of the civil war in Holland.

As regards social standing, Hildegard von Bingen of Germany was nearly as influential during the 1100s as her illustrious contemporary, St. Bernard. Byzantium elevated several women to positions of supreme power, while in the West after 1400, Isabella of Spain, Elizabeth I of England, Maria Theresa of Austria, and Victoria of England made a record that no male foursome can match. Prior to 1400, women often ruled in lieu of sons and husbands as, for example, Margaret of Scotland (wife of Malcolm), Blanche of

---

[71]   William Barclay, *The Gospel of Luke* (1975), 17.

Castille (mother of Louis IX), Matilda of Normandy (wife of William the conqueror), Ximena of Valencia (wife of El Cid), and Juana of Spain (sister of Philip II).

Although the daughters of the Roman nobility could be highly cultured — one thinks of St. Paula, Jerome's collaborator — female education seems to have received an extra fillip with the advent of Christianity. During the darkest period of the so-called "Dark Ages," Hilda, abbess of Whitby, governed a fiefdom that included monks, as well as nuns, and such an arrangement was not uncommon. Internationally renowned for her learning, as well as her charity, Hilda became the patron of England's first native poet, Caedmon. As an advisor to bishops, as well as princes and kings, she also hosted the Great Synod of 644. Other examples of intellectually distinguished women drawn from the pages of early history include Elburga, Radegund, Agnes, Mildred, and Audrey.

During the Middle Ages, women inherited large estates and received as much, if not more, education than their male siblings. Thus Margaret was better educated than Malcolm. Mary, the wife of Philip II, and Isabel of Portugal, who married Charles V of Spain, were again more learned than their husbands. And so it was perfectly natural for Charles to listen to his wife in preference to other royal councilors and for her to take charge of the kingdom during his long absences.[72]

If the male owner of a medieval business died, it was customary for his wife to step in. Likewise, most guilds admitted women, offered them the same benefits as men, and outfitted them in the same kind of livery.

There were female professors of Greek, Latin, and rhetoric at leading universities such as Salamanca and Alcalá at the time of Isabella.[73] Small wonder that Catherine of Siena and Teresa of Avila have been judged worthy to share the title "Doctor of the Church" with such luminaries as Augustine and Thomas Aquinas.

---

[72] Windeat biography, 29, 105; William Thomas Walsh, *Philip II*, 3, 136, 138.
[73] Walsh, *Isabella*, 248.

Christian Charity

Dramatic gains for women were accompanied by an equally novel concern for outcasts. Christ's compassion for the poor, disabled, and sick led to the founding of orphanages, hospitals, and homes for the aged — something hitherto unheard of. In heathen Sparta, when a child was born, its fate was submitted to a board of examiners, and only if healthy was it permitted to go on living. Any sign of weakness or deformity meant automatic exposure to death on a mountainside.

It was Thalasius, a Christian monk, who founded the world's first asylum for the blind. Fabiola, a Christian lady, was responsible for the first hospital on record, and Apollonius, a Christian merchant, established the first free dispensary.[74]

One might add that today's International Red Cross owes its existence to the work of Jean Henri Dunant, a pioneer in the World Evangelical Alliance and World Union of Young Men's Christian Associations. Dunant also spearheaded the arbitration movement and Hague Court system and, in conjunction with Frederic Passy, became the first person to win a Nobel Peace Prize.

Returning to the Middle Ages, Louis IX of France, under whose patronage the Sorbonne was founded, established two free libraries, one for the students of Notre Dame, another at the Louvre for the general public. So vast, in fact, were Louis' charitable enterprises, which included three hospitals, along with institutes for reforming prostitutes and training the blind, that it alarmed his court. Yet this was not unusual for the time. Just as a bishop of Paris during the 12th century established a special hospital for unfortunates (the Hotel Dieu or "God's Hospice") under the supervision of Augustinian nuns, so too did Francis of Assisi embrace a leper for the greater glory of God.

Neither were prisoners of war forgotten. Peter Nolasco, tutor to Juan of Aragon, founded the Order of the Blessed Virgin Mary for the ransom of captives in 1218. Members of the Order, generally laymen pledged to poverty, chastity, and obedience, vowed to devote their whole substance and, if need be, their very lives to the

---

[74] William Barclay, *The Gospel of Matthew* (1975), II, 80.

welfare and release of captives. An estimated 2,700 individuals were ransomed during Nolasco's lifetime, followed by another 70,000 over the years.

A great many bishops and abbots were genuinely holy men during the early Middle Ages, and the legacy continued.[75] Several hundred years later, Milan's archbishop Charles Borromeo not only founded schools for the poor but also risked his life for his flock. Refusing to leave town during the devastating plague of 1576, he never ceased caring for the sick and dying, going so far as to sell his bed for their support. One wonders how many congressmen, senators, educators, or social workers nowadays would be willing to do the same.

Monasteries offered free hospitality to travelers and the destitute; and monks, as well as nuns, ran schools for gifted children of parents without means. Free schooling, supported as early as 451 by the Council of Chalcedon, was gradually extended to the higher rungs of the academic ladder so that by the time of Isabella, universities such as Salamanca, Spain's finest, welcomed scholarship students.

It is easy to forget, in addition, what a powerful effect Christianity had on the status of workingmen. Aristotle viewed manual labor as degrading, and Plato regarded tradesmen as contemptible. Accordingly, these classes were excluded from the Roman Forum when the high priest offered sacrifice, and manual labor was performed almost exclusively by slaves. Such thinking became dated the moment St. Benedict converted his cloister into a workshop.

In time, a whole system of social security superior to anything that succeeded it came into being with the formation of the medieval guilds. Never before or since have workingmen been so highly regarded or so well protected. Expenses relating to unemployment, illness, and old age — even funeral fees and the cost of pilgrimages — were underwritten by employers and the guilds on behalf of apprentices, journeymen, and masters. Customers could count on quality craftsmanship and guarantees of personal character, while guild members, for their part, were generous with time and

---

[75] McManners, ed., *Oxford Illustrated History*, 119.

money, visiting prisoners and donating dowries to girls from indigent families.[76]

To be sure, serfs were tied to the land and beholden to their master, and vassals paid homage to a feudal lord. But masters and lords had obligations of their own, not least of which was the duty to furnish armor, cavalry, and leadership in time of war.

How could Christians fail to appreciate the dignity of labor when Peter, Andrew, James, and John were fishermen and Paul a tent-maker? Jesus was, of course, a carpenter who upbraided one of his dinner hosts for not inviting a broad enough cross section of society.[77] In recent times, Britain's Labour Party, as well as its trade union movement, were "virtually born in the chapel."[78]

Christian notions of equality and brotherhood had implications far transcending the cloister. If one were to trace the influence of Jesus on the rise of egalitarianism, one would have to compare the progress of democracy in the Christian West with the prevalence of absolutism in Asia and the Far East. England's Magna Carta was the product of lobbying by bishops in league with nobles; and it was on church lands that serfs first gained their freedom as a matter of right. When Pope Leo XIII, in his encyclical *Rerum Novarum* (1891), upheld the dignity of labor and the right of working men and women to a living (family) wage, he was merely adhering to age-old Catholic tradition.

In the Final Analysis

When all the evidence has been sifted and weighed, the case for Christianity, like that for belief in a divine being, is not going to overwhelm a determined skeptic. God has taken too many precautions to ensure the element of free will. He is careful to allow just enough room for doubt, just enough of an aperture for disbelief, so that the final choice between good and evil, truth and falsehood, remains ours.

---

[76] Much of this material on medieval life is derived from a magnificent volume by James J. Walsh: *The Thirteenth, Greatest of Centuries* (1952).

[77] Luke 14:12-14.

[78] Gertrude Himmelfarb, *The De-Moralization of Society* (1995), 255.

Each year, readers devour best sellers by the millions on every conceivable subject without ever picking up a biography of the world's most fascinating and influential person. And they are within their rights. Jesus experienced the same kind of studied indifference at the hands of the literati.

Still, every man is born with a conscience which impels him to search out the truth. And Christianity *is* the truth. In the words of Our Savior: "I am the way, the truth, and the life" (John 14:6). Cases of invincible ignorance there may be. But they are rare, one would suppose, in an age of mass media, especially in western culture. "If I had not come," Christ said, and "done among them works such as no one else has done, they would have no sin," but "now they have no excuse for their sin" (John 15:22-25). This was the challenge to the people of his day that took Jesus all the way to Calvary, and it most certainly has a claim on each and every one of us.[79]

---

[79] On belief in Jesus, once exposed to his teaching, as a requirement for salvation, see Acts 3:22; 13:48; 18:6; Mk. 16:16; Luke 10:10-16.

Chapter 3

The Case for Catholicism

The Church that took possession of Rome after Constantine and went on to transform pagan society, the Church that labored to improve the lot of slaves, workingmen, women, the ill, aged, and ignorant, the Church whose members erected cathedrals, discovered the New World, beat off the threat of Islam, and achieved preeminence internationally in the field of artistic and technical endeavor was Catholic to the core. It worshiped Christ as God, celebrated Mass, heard confessions, invoked the saints, venerated relics, and looked to the Holy Father for guidance on spiritual matters. Then came the Protestant Reformation. A variety of autonomous sects laid claim to God's special favor, and the course was set.

Presently, we shall deal with such topics as the Crusades, the Spanish Inquisition, Galileo, and the Nazi Holocaust. But first, a brief overview of some of the more immediate consequences of rebellion against papal authority.

Morals and the Reformation

The man whose nailing of ninety-five theses to the door of Wittenberg Cathedral acted as a catalyst for widespread defection was Martin Luther, and it should be said at the outset that his translation of the Bible into German did not make it accessible to the common man, as is often assumed. The average person of Luther's time could not read or write; and among those who could, almost all understood Latin. Luther was not even the first to translate scripture into the vernacular. Nine German editions appeared before his birth; there were dozens more by the time he published his own, and we are speaking only of Germany. Italian scholars put out more than forty Catholic editions of the Bible in their native tongue before the appearance of the first Protestant version.[80]

If Luther is important, it is due to the impact of his ideas on German conduct, for it was not long before areas under Protestant control began to show signs of moral slippage. Luther himself approved of bigamy, justifying it in the case of Philip of Hesse on Old Testament grounds; and he went to his grave lamenting the fact that Wittenberg, the birthplace of Protestantism, had become "worse than Sodom."[81] Men, he wrote, were "more vindictive, more greedy, more pitiless, more immoral and unrestrained and much more evil than they were under the papacy."[82]

Philip Melanchthon, another reformer, was of like mind, while Erasmus, the most celebrated scholar of his time, remarked that "wherever Luther prevails, the cause of literature and learning is lost."[83] Three centuries later, Protestant historian Adolf Harnack acknowledged that "since the beginning of the Reformation, one must deplore the relaxed morality of the German churches and the lack of seriousness in the work of sanctification."[84]

Among other things, Luther was virulently anti-Semitic. His tract, "On the Jews and their Lies," refers to them as "poisonous envenomed worms" whose synagogues "should be set on fire … [their homes] smashed and destroyed" [and their people] "put under one roof or in a stable like gypsies to teach them they are not master in our land."[85]

In London, we find Henry VIII, on the aftermath of the English Reformation, in his last speech to Parliament, regretting "how

---

[80]   Henry Graham, *Where We Got the Bible* (1987 reprint), 105; Paul Stenhouse, *Catholic Answers to "Bible" Christians* (1993), I, 4-5.

[81]   James Cardinal Gibbons, *The Faith of Our Fathers* (1980 reprint), 302-306, 340; Robert D. Smith, *The Mark of Holiness* (1961), 254; Walsh, *Philip II*, 78.

[82]   Smith, *The Mark of Holiness*, 254.

[83]   Robert Fox, *A Catechism of the Catholic Church* (1979), 129.

[84]   Smith, *Mark of Holiness*, 254.

[85]   Paul Johnson, *A History of the Jews* (paperback), 242.

much the word of God is abused; with how little reverence it is mentioned, how people squabble about the sense [of scripture] ... I am sure charity was never in a more languishing condition, virtue never at a lower ebb, nor God himself less honoured or worse served in Christendom."[86] English witchcraft trials, resulting in the execution of an estimated 30,000, exceeded the worst excesses of the Spanish Inquisition.

Not all Protestant commentators would agree with Luther, Melanchthon, Erasmus, and Henry. Still, there is ample cause for concern. Protestants introduced the gruesome practice of giving no quarter and taking no prisoners of war.[87] And if the scholars Westermarck and Ottiger are correct, the suicide rate for Protestants was twice that of Catholics on a per capita basis, even as rates rose to disproportionate levels in other areas such as abortion and illegitimacy.[88]

By the middle of the nineteenth century, the moral dichotomy between Catholics and Protestants appears to have widened. The *Journal* of the Statistical Society of London for the years 1860, 1862, 1865, and 1867 put illegitimacy in England and Wales at 6.5 per hundred, as compared with a rate in Catholic Ireland of only 3 per hundred.[89] The *Scotsman*, whose reports were based on the British Registrar-General, published similar findings on illegitimacy: Ireland 3.8%, England 6.4%, Scotland 9.9%.[90] Ralph Waldo Emerson had it from Carlyle and Dickens at a dinner party that male chastity was as good as gone in England — so rare, in fact, that one could name all the exceptions.[91]

Throughout the twentieth century, it is Protestant Scandinavia, Sweden in particular, that one associates with the flouting of family values. In England, after requirements for divorce were reduced to mutual consent, rates soared, becoming the highest in Europe. Other statistics tell much the same story. Divorce rates in Canada,

---

[86] Graham, *Where We Got the Bible*, 136-37.
[87] Walsh, *Philip II*, 536.
[88] Smith, *Mark of Holiness*, 255.
[89] Gibbons, *Faith of Our Fathers*, 303.
[90] Ibid., 304.
[91] Emerson diary, quoted in Paul Johnson, *Intellectuals*, 140.

the United States, and Australia — all former British colonies — are the highest internationally.[92] England is second to the United States in teenage illegitimacy, and the British per capita crime rate in 1995 was ten times that of 1955, sixty times that of 1900.[93]

Much has been made of allegations of political corruption south of the Rio Grande. Such charges would be telling were it not for the fact that the formation of the public sector in many of the nations of Latin America has been heavily influenced by Uncle Sam. Democracy is hardly a homegrown product in Spanish and Portuguese-speaking regions of the world, nor can one assume that it is even the preference of a majority of the people. If, therefore, it appears lacking in refinement, the fault may lie less with people on the local level than with their North American mentors whose criticism has been less than sporting.

The taking of mistresses, another practice associated with Catholic countries where divorce is illegal, is often cited as an equalizer. But there is a difference between marital dissolution and marital infidelity. Both are tragic and both, certainly, have serious consequences. But one is primary in the way it affects spouse and offspring, the other secondary.

Protestant America leads the world in abortion, illegitimacy, teenage suicide, crime, and divorce. The U.S. crime rate trebled between 1965 and 1990, with Canada and Australia not far behind.[94] America also ranks near the bottom of the industrialized world in the caliber of its students. Even its best are notably inferior. The Netherlands, another child of the Reformation, became the first nation to afford legal protection to assisted suicide while Australia and the United States were close runners-up.

The Czech Republic, another case in point, is divided into a predominantly Protestant area in the west (Bohemia) and an area to the east that is mostly Catholic (Moravia). Bohemia has four to five times as many abortions as Moravia.[95]

---

[92] The Episcopal Church in America moved as early as 1973 to allow remarriage after divorce (see *The New York Times*, September 23, 1982, p. A20).

[93] Thatcher, *Path to Power*, 541; Himmelfarb, *De-Moralization*, 224.

[94] Thatcher, *Path to Power*, 541; *Wall Street Journal*, February 25, 1998 ("Why America Has the World's Dimmest Bright Kids").

[95] *Human Life Reports*, November 1997, p. 7.

The 1930 Lambeth Conference of Anglicans was the first such conclave to approve artificial contraception; and since then, Protestant leaders have sanctioned euthanasia, as well as abortion. Currently, the Episcopal Church of America is reeling from a 30% decline in membership in as many years. A divorced woman was recently consecrated bishop and there have been celebrations by the Episcopal clergy of "gay" marriage. It is all of a piece.

Society and the Reformation

Dramatic as the impact of Christian schism appears to have been on morals, the full extent of its influence cannot be assessed without calculating its effect on the lives of the world's unfortunates.

When Henry VIII abolished the monasteries, there was no agency qualified to take their place in the business of relieving destitution and nursing the sick. The Reformation was also hard on peasants who had to face rapidly escalating prices without any appreciable increase in wages. Many were driven off monastic common lands to make room for a rising middle class bent upon consolidating farm operations for maximum profit. Consequently, a whole new class of beggars materialized. Prize-winning historian William Thomas Walsh put it succinctly:

> Another result ... [of the Reformation] in England had been the reduction of the mass of the people to a state of poverty unknown in Spain at that time or in medieval England. Not only had the small farmers been dispossessed from monastery lands so that such families as Bacon's could make more money raising sheep; not only did the national and city governments fail to give alms to the poor, the disabled and the insane, who had been cared for by the monks and nuns; not only was the Catholic hospital system in the Middle Ages shattered [along] with the Guilds, which had established an equilibrium of employer and workman; but poor wretches, deprived of a livelihood and of any possibility of finding one, were then punished for their

misfortune by inhuman laws, cruelly enforced. The Act of 1573 provided that a beggar should be bored through the ears and whipped, and at the third offense put to death. The Middlesex Sessions Rolls record the branding and whipping of seventy-one vagrants in two months in 1591.[96]

This was the age of Elizabeth, who dispensed with the custom of washing feet from the throne on Holy Thursday, agreeing at first to bathe the feet of those already cleansed, then abandoning the practice altogether.[97]

Three centuries later, conditions for many of England's workers were, as one might expect, substandard. Nowhere else in the world were entrepreneurs so free to operate as they saw fit. Subsistence wages, grinding hours, child labor, workhouses, and debtor prisons were all a part of the picture. Few who have read Dickens are likely to forget Oliver Twist's plaintive cry, "Please, Sir, may I have some more?" Alexis de Tocqueville, writing in 1833, observed that "the countries appearing to be the most impoverished are those which in reality account for the fewest indigent, and among the people most admired for their opulence, one part of the population is obliged to rely on the gifts of the other in order to live." Worse, though, than the poverty was the stigma attached to it, especially when one landed in a workhouse. As Disraeli quipped, poverty in England was "a crime."[98]

Colonization

Max Weber, author of *The Protestant Ethic and the Spirit of Capitalism*, might well have written a sequel entitled, *The Protestant Ethic and Slavery*. After the Orthodox (Byzantine) split with Rome in 1054, slavery continued to flourish in schismatic and Muslim areas of the East while virtually disappearing in the West

---

[96] Walsh, *Philip II*, 633 (also 142, 546, 632).
[97] See *This Rock*, May, 1995, p. 4. Philip II of Spain, meanwhile, continued the practice – see Walsh, *Philip II*, 577.
[98] Himmelfarb, *De-Moralization*, 125 (Tocqueville) and 133 (Disraeli).

under papal influence. Following the Reformation, England became the principal importer of slaves. Meanwhile, a crusade led by Montesquieu and an impassioned priest by the name of Abbé Gregoire forced the abolition of slavery in the French empire, albeit temporarily.[99] A French island, Haiti, became the first Caribbean possession to guarantee freedom to all its people. And it was not long before Brazil, Colombia, and Mexico followed suit.[100]

A comparative analysis of imperial slave codes reveals a number of striking differences.[101] France and Spain, unlike England, limited the prerogatives of owners (in 1685 and 1789 respectively). Unlike their brethren to the north, Latin American chattel could earn their freedom after a reasonable term of service. They also had rights to leisure and reception of the sacraments. At the same time, priests acting as monitors in the name of King and Church insisted on church marriage, along with guarantees against selling families apart. By comparison, slaves in certain Protestant areas were actually barred from entering a binding marriage.

Portuguese, Spanish, and French colonizers exhibited remarkably little color prejudice. Interracial marriage was often encouraged; and in not a few areas, because it was the custom for the fathers of miscegenous unions to free their offspring in conjunction with the mother, a class of free and relatively prosperous mulattoes emerged, Haiti being the prime example. British spheres, on the other hand, tended to make miscegenation extremely difficult when they did not prohibit it altogether. Thus, when Latin America was "liberated" from Spanish rule by native forces in league with Protestant allies in the early 1800s, mixed marriage was forbidden. Likewise, when the Philippines was occupied by the United States in 1898, Filipinos visiting North America found that they were proscribed by law from marrying into white society.

Naturally, the Spanish had their share of opportunists, men who were venal and rapacious and who committed atrocities. It is just that there were powerful countervailing forces at work which in the long run proved decisive. In 1550, Madrid took the unprec-

---

[99] *Encyclopaedia Britannica* (1973), XX, 634.

[100] Most of the above facts are contained in the *Encyclopaedia Britannica* (1973), XX, 634 ff.

[101] See Stanley Elkins, *Slavery*; also *Encyclopaedia Britannica* (1973), XX, 635.

edented step of suspending all military activity in America pending the results of an inquiry into the conduct of Spanish colonizers. There were frequent inspections by the officers of both crown and Church; and governors, as a matter of course, ran the gauntlet of royal investigation at the end of every term.

Spanish policy governing the Indians was again remarkably liberal for its time, having no use for eviction or consignment to reservations, again in marked contrast to practices common in North America. Neither the mother country nor the Church ever resorted to forced conversion. Prior to the miraculous occurrences at Guadalupe, Mexico (1531), relatively few among the natives had been anxious to convert. Likewise in the case of Peru, where few Indians embraced the faith until Rose of Lima appeared on the scene. Professor Walsh describes the treatment accorded native Filipinos by Philip II of Spain:

> He found there a semi-savage people. Instead of exterminating them, as the English were to exterminate the aborigines of North America ... [Spanish officials] patiently taught them Christianity and the arts of civilization, introduced better methods of rice culture, brought Indian corn and cacao from America, developed the growth of indigo, coffee and sugar cane, united the people to the stream of Christian European culture by helping them to learn Spanish, and encouraged their natural love of music. Philip authorized the Jesuits to found a college there in 1585, though it was not opened until 1601. The College of Saint Potenciana for girls was established in 1593. A century and a half after his death, there would be nearly a million Christian souls on the island in 569 parishes. Even in his lifetime, it was evident that Spain had raised a half-savage people to a relatively high standard of civilization, and this not by force or exploitation or political chicanery, but principally by patient labors of priests and monks; by Christian charity. This is indisputable. Philip otherwise could never have held the islands with a garrison of only 400 men,

to protect them from Sulus, Moslems and Chinese and Dutch pirates.[102]

The Philippines remains the only Christian nation in the Far East. Another feature of Spanish imperial policy that stands out in sharp relief is the degree to which it tolerated criticism. Las Casas, Vitoria, Montesinos, and others were free to deplore the moral consequences of imperial expansion, and they did.

Vitoria, a Dominican theologian at Salamanca and one of the founding fathers of international law, was outraged by Pizarro's methods in Peru, and over the years, his writings, along with those of other advocates of Indian rights such as Las Casas, had a profound impact, not only on scholars and theologians, but also on government officials, resulting in a series of reforms promulgated by Charles I and succeeding monarchs. The Indians, Vitoria insisted, must never be made to suffer in order that Spain might prosper.

Prominent among the champions of the rights of Indians and slaves in the New World were Juan de Zumárraga, the first bishop of Mexico; José de Anchieta, S. J., apostle to Brazil and the father of Brazilian literature; Archbishop Turibius of Lima, who succeeded in having slavery abolished; Father Francisco Solano, the Franciscan hero of Indian folk song; Blessed Junipero Serra of California; Diego Vargas of Santa Fe; and three viceroys of New Spain: Don Antonio de Mendoza, Velasco, and Buscareli. The Jesuits, for their part, established communities in Paraguay (present-day Argentina, Uruguay, Paraguay, and part of Brazil) — "reductions," as they were called — where the Indians were secure, well cared for, and happy.

The Black Legend

Abuses of power by Spanish overlords there were. But they have been exaggerated. Although the owners of plantation fiefdoms called "encomiendas" were known to take unfair advantage of their Indian laborers, the encomienda system was promptly abolished, and whatever its problems, they were embroidered by reform-minded writers in an attempt to bring about change. Little did domestic critics suspect at the time that Spain's overseas enemies would

---

[102] Walsh, *Philip II*, 714.

weave homegrown propaganda into what has come to be known as "the Black Legend," a hostile and heavily slanted account of Spanish government.

Black Legend history touches lightly, if at all, on the fact that the Indians encountered by conquistadors were far from humane and peace-loving. Columbus, on reaching San Salvador, was greeted by the remnant of a tribe that had been literally eaten alive by its neighbors, the Caribs. And when Pizarro reached Peru, the Incas had just flung the bodies of 20,000 members of a rival tribe into a lake.[103]

In Mexico and Guatemala, Mayan cities spent much of their time at war, and the Aztec empire was one of the world's cruellest. After conquering neighboring tribes, officials loaded their subjects with taxes and demanded human victims for sacrifice to the gods. Some of these victims were prisoners of war, but not all. Aztec law required a thousand human sacrifices annually from every town with a temple. There were 371 subject towns and the total number of killings every year is said to have been in the vicinity of 50,000.

The early Mexican historian, Ixtilxochitl, estimated that one out of every five children in Mexico died in this manner. According to Professor Carroll, entire tribes numbering in the tens of thousands were "on several occasions exterminated by sacrifice." Carroll goes on to say that "the most feared and evil leader in the later days of the empire was Tllacaellel, who, on the occasion of dedicating a new pyramid-temple in 1487, according to chroniclers at that time, sacrificed between 20,000 and 80,000 men in a period of four days.[104]

Black Legend historians have charged that killer diseases such as tuberculosis were brought to America by the Spanish. But the recent discovery of a body belonging to a Peruvian woman buried a thousand years ago suggests that tubercular germs were already present in the New World when Columbus arrived.[105] In any event, Indians were not the only victims of disease. Within four years of De Soto's landing on the coast of Florida with a thousand men (1538), he himself, along with most of his party, had succumbed to germs.

Finally, readers of the Black Legend are not likely to learn that the Spanish Crown supported schools for the children of poor Indi-

---

[103] Robert E. Smith, *The Other Side of Christ*, 23.

[104] Warren Carroll, "Our Lady of Guadalupe and the Conquest of Darkness."

[105] *Wall Street Journal*, March 15, 1984, p. 15.

ans and that, unlike English sovereigns, it would not permit its overseas colonies to be used as a dumping ground for men and women with criminal records. Within thirteen years of the conquest of Mexico, the first institution of higher education, Holy Cross College, opened its doors to Indians. Nineteen years later, there were two more colleges in addition to a university. Native Mexicans of Indian extraction would soon be crossing the Atlantic to teach in the universities of Europe.

Catholicism in Action

All of which brings us full circle to the question of how Catholicism has contributed in recent centuries to the betterment of mankind. The story, which at this point is largely biographical, begins with a gallery of names. Peter Claver (1580-1654) and Joseph de Veuster (better known as Father Damien, 1840-89) stand out for their effort to assist slaves and lepers respectively, and both were priests. It was Louis Braille (1809-52), a devout French Catholic, who designed the special alphabet for the blind which still bears his name, while Abbé de L'Epée, a French monk, is the father of sign language. Still another Frenchman, Laurent Clerc, himself deaf, was the first to teach deaf mutes in America. In 1817, he joined with Thomas Gallaudet to launch the American School for the Deaf in Hartford, Connecticut.

Elizabeth Ann Seton, the first native-born citizen of the United States to be canonized and foundress of the Catholic parochial school system, established a religious order, the Sisters of Charity, which grew so fast that in less than a hundred years, 10,000 of its sisters were operating not only schools but also 150 hospitals, along with foundling homes, sanitariums, Black and Indian institutes, and a refuge for lepers.[106]

Catholic sisters opened the first American military hospital (in New Orleans), the first free school west of the Mississippi, and the world-famous Mayo Clinic in Rochester, Minnesota. During the Civil War, 600 Sisters of Loretto nursed wounded soldiers on the front lines where few of their sex had ever ventured. Boys'

---

[106] Alma Power-Waters, *Mother Seton*, 186.

Town in Nebraska was founded by Father Flanagan; and a nun, Katherine Drexel, risked her life to found the first secondary school for Blacks in the post-Civil War South. "Mother Katherine," as she was called, began her apostolate with a small group of followers, and when she died in 1955 at the age of 97, she left behind almost 600 Sisters of the Blessed Sacrament with forty-nine convents and sixty-one schools for Indians and Blacks, including Xavier University in New Orleans.[107]

Until recently, the vast majority of American Catholics were first or second generation immigrants of modest means. Few in number relative to the overall population and frequently lacking in educational and cultural background, they nonetheless contributed 250,000 vocations to the priesthood and religious life prior to 1965, which in turn made possible the staffing of 304 colleges and universities, 10,500 parochial schools, 2,455 high schools, 950 hospitals and sanitoria, 250 orphanages, and 257 homes for the aged.[108]

When it comes to overseas relief work, there is, of course, Mother Teresa of Calcutta, winner of the Nobel Peace Prize. After taking thousands of hungry, homeless, and dying off the streets of Calcutta and caring for them lovingly, she and her sisters opened 500 hospitals, clinics, hostels, and youth centers in over a hundred countries.

Today, Mother Teresa's parent organization, the Catholic Church, runs 22,000 health-care facilities around the world.[109]

Catholicism and the Arts

The fruit of Catholicism is not confined to social work. It cannot be denied that Protestant countries made great strides in finance, colonization, and government, fields driven by a spirit of

---

[107] Biography by Ellen Tarry, 189.
[108] Stewart, *Marvels of Charity*, 449.
[109] *Human Life International Reports*, August 1994, p. 9. Also interesting in this connection is the fact that India's Dalits (or "untouchables"), who make up 60% of the population, have received far more sympathy and help from Catholics than from Protestants (see *Catholic World Report*, October 1997, p. 49).

acquisitiveness — London became a center of banking and insurance, Amsterdam a hub of trade and commerce. But is was to Paris and Vienna that leaders in the area of visual and musical design gravitated. Northern Germany, more prosperous and less Catholic than southern Germany, was also less artistic.

In music, the classical repertoire is overwhelmingly Catholic: Palestrina, Monteverdi, Vivaldi, Corelli (the father of modern violin playing), Haydn, Mozart, Franck (the father of modern harmony), Beethoven, Gounod, Debussy, Saint-Saens, Fauré, Elgar, Mahler (a convert), and Bruckner. Franz Schubert, Giuseppe Verdi, Frederic Chopin, and Antonin Dvorak were products of traditional Catholic upbringing; and Franz Liszt, who wrote a treatise on music and religion which influenced his son-in-law, Richard Wagner, dreamed in his younger days of becoming a priest.

Bach, Brahms, Schumann, Mendelssohn, and Wagner were Protestants, as were Sibelius and Grieg, and their greatness is beyond question. Tchaikovsky, Mussorgsky, and Rimsky-Korsakov belonged to the communion of Russian Orthodox. Still, the great preponderance of musical talent and output lies on the Catholic side. One might add that Tchaikovsky, Rimsky-Korsakov, and Mendelssohn were inspired to write some of their finest works, including the *Capriccio Italien*, *Capriccio Español*, and the *Italian Symphony*, during visits to Catholic countries.

While "low church" Protestants were stripping away visual effects and eliminating music from the weekly service, while English carolers were having a lean time under Elizabeth — "Merrie Old England" was merry no longer — French composers were turning out Christmas carols called "Noels," among them "O Holy Night." "Silent Night," incidentally, was the work of an Austrian priest in collaboration with his organist.

Opera sprang from Italy, ballet from Italy and France, and it is no coincidence that New Orleans, most Catholic of southern cities, became the cradle of America's best-known musical invention, jazz. Calypso, a mix of Spanish, Creole, and African musical idiom, may be traced to Trinidad at the start of the nineteenth century when the island was predominantly Catholic. Britain didn't take possession until 1797, and many of the barbed lyrics associated with Calypso took aim at the island's new rulers.

In the field of painting and sculpture, the city whose name comes most readily to mind is Florence. Michelangelo, Leonardo da Vinci, Giotto and Della Robbia were products of Catholic culture, as were Van Dyck and Rubens. Spain produced Velázquez, Murillo, and Goya, while the most important nineteenth century school of painting, Impressionism, originated in France under the inspiration of a devout Catholic, Jean-Baptiste Camille Corot. Paul Cézanne, another distinguished painter, attended daily Mass.

Next in order of artistry come the crafts, and among the leaders here are Irish crystal (Waterford), French fashion and cuisine, Italian leatherwork, Belgian tapestry, and French lace (St. Thérèse of Lisieux's mother, herself a candidate for sainthood, was the premier lace maker of Alençon, France's principal lace center). Stradiveri, whose violins are still the greatest of all prizes for a string virtuoso, was an Italian Catholic who is said to have remarked, "If my hand slacked, I should rob God."[110]

If one had been a guest in 1794 at the home of William Seton, senior partner in the New York shipping firm bearing his name and a pillar of the Episcopal Church, one would have found tapestries from Florence, chandeliers from Rome, and carpets from Spain. Mr. Seton's coat was of French cut and his shirt collar of Michelin lace.[111] One can go further. The most renowned linguist of all time, a man fluent in thirty-nine languages, was a prince of the Church, Cardinal Mezzofanti (b. 1774). Alexis de Tocqueville, a Frenchman who left the Church but later returned, penned the most incisive of all commentaries on American culture and politics. And in the world of cinema, Alfred Hitchcock, Alec Guinness, Helen Hayes, John Wayne, Gary Cooper, John Ford, and Frank Capra (of *It's a Wonderful Life* and *Mr. Smith Goes to Washington* fame) all had one thing in common: their faith. Either they were born in the Church or they entered it as adults. Likewise, the most popular movie ever made, *Gone With the Wind*, is based on a novel by Margaret Mitchell. Mitchell was reared by a brilliant mother whose apostolic zeal and love for the Church led to the conversion of Margaret's father.[112]

---

[110] William Barclay, *The Acts of the Apostles*, 45.
[111] Power-Waters, *Mother Seton*, 36.
[112] Margaret Mitchell herself fell away from the faith while at Smith College.

A Spirit of Joy

"These things I have spoken to you," said Jesus, "that my joy may be in you and that your joy may be made full ... Your hearts will rejoice with a joy no one can take from you" (John 15:11; 16:23). At the conclusion of the Last Supper, as Our Lord was about to make his way to the Garden of Gethsemane in what must have been an agony of anticipation, he led his followers in song (Mk. 14:26). Paul, in like vein, exhorted his band to "rejoice in the Lord always, again I say rejoice!" (Phil. 4:4). Clearly, joy was a prized possession of the early Christian community, and the question is where one is most likely to find it today. Proverbial expressions such as "sunny Italy" and "the Irish smile" may be indicative, coupled with the fact that Filipinos are in such great demand around the world as nurses and doctors owing to the therapeutic effect of a cheerful disposition. But returning to music, few strains are more contagiously jubilant than those of the Mexican pastorela. The music of the mariachi band, so full of exuberance, is again Mexican. Vienna, city of carefree gaiety, gave us the waltz. Flamenco is from Seville; and the tango, cha-cha, rhumba, samba, and merengue all trace their origin to places south of the Rio Grande. How many dances of comparable panache have come out of London, Edinburgh, Stockholm, or Copenhagen since the time of the Reformation?

A Special Regard for Children

Shifting to still another theme, that of Catholicism and children, one recalls that Jesus entered the world as an infant and that his love for children was boundless. "Let the little ones come to me," he pleaded: "It is not the will of your father in heaven that one of these little ones should perish" (Mt.18:10-14; 19:13-15). He wrapped his arms around youngsters, blessed them, and extolled them as models of faith.

Here again, one must ask which religious group is mostly deeply imbued with this particular charism. Which nations are in the vanguard of those that welcome children? Household words like La Leche, Lamaze, and Cuisenaire (Cuisenaire rods) point in the direction of France and Spain, particularly the former. Early in the

1800s, a path-breaking institute for deaf mutes was founded in Paris by Pereire. Itard, a French physician, was the first to study retarded students on a scientific basis, much the way hospital cases are observed today; and Seguin, another Frenchman, designed the first comprehensive educational program for retarded children.

Many of the most advanced techniques in elementary education can be traced to Maria Montessori, Italy's first woman doctor and a committed Catholic, who built on the work of Itard and Seguin. Pint-sized tables and chairs, three-dimensional geometric puzzles, beads designed to instill mathematical concepts, and Cuisenaire rods are all part of the Montessori method. Likewise, the modern playground configuration in conjunction with learning centers, open classrooms, and the concept of "magnet" or "alternative" schools. The Montessori approach to teaching, with its emphasis on order, repetition, the senses, hands-on manipulation and exploration for the sake of developing independence, has been adopted by schools everywhere.

France was not only the cradle of children's literature during the seventeenth and eighteenth centuries. It was also the birthplace of Charles Perrault's fairy tales, "Sleeping Beauty," "Cinderella," and "Little Red Riding Hood." "Beauty and the Beast," as we know it, was introduced into England by a Frenchwoman, Mme. Marie Leprince de Beaumont (1711-80). And *Mother Goose's Tales*, along with *Mother Bunch's Fairy Tales*, originated in France as well. Another Frenchman by the name of Fenelon (1651-1750) published a version of Homer for children that positively captivated the English and remained standard fare on both sides of the Channel for over a hundred years. Finally, modern science fiction, so appealing to children, began with Jules Verne, French author of *Twenty Thousand Leagues Under the Sea* and *Around the World in Eighty Days*.

The Crusades

This said, the thoughtful reader may wonder if it is not time to shift focus for a moment and look at the Crusades, the Spanish Inquisition, the Church's response to Galileo, and the Nazi Holocaust, topics widely perceived as putting the Church in a less than favorable light. The answer is yes.

Critics of the Crusades tend to emphasize their futility (Jerusalem could not be held) coupled with the unedifying spectacle of gentlemen warriors killing in the name of religion. Hideous acts of pillage and rapine are retailed. The plunder of Constantinople by western soldiers during the Fourth Crusade is said to have embittered Eastern Orthodox leaders beyond all hope of reconciliation, while tales of merchants selling youngsters into slavery in Egypt during the so-called Children's Crusade are bruited.

Much of this may be true. But the picture is incomplete. Crusaders did not fight for the sake of fighting. Neither did they take the field to force conversion. Muslims had massacred Christian sojourners, razed the Church of the Holy Sepulcher (1009), closed Jerusalem to pilgrims (1072), and seized Edessa. Excesses there were, and not all of the principals were virtuous. Crusaders like Bohemond and Charles of Anjou were grasping and ruthless. Others, however — men like Godfrey of Bouillon and Louis IX — exhibited a spirit of self-sacrifice and behaved gallantly. Europe's best and brightest fought in the Crusades or worked to promote them: St. Edward the Confessor of England, St. Bernard of Clairvaux, and St. Francis of Assisi, to name a few.

It has become commonplace to kill for political causes. Few in the West care enough about religion these days to discuss it, much less fight over it. One is therefore hard put to imagine an era when people everywhere regarded faith as paramount, when saints and sinners alike viewed church and state as virtually one and the same, and when some of history's most valiant generals and kings fought to oust the infidel. Do we condemn Joshua, Asa, Josiah, or Jehosaphat for moving to eradicate idolatry? Do we think less of Elijah for executing false prophets by the hundreds?

The responsible historian will, of necessity, entertain a wide range of questions. For instance: was a more relaxed attitude possible at a time when Islam seemed on the verge of world conquest? Muslim chieftains had marched into France in 778 A.D., only to be repulsed; but the menace remained. An eastern offensive in 1683 would carry knights of the crescent all the way to the gates of Vienna. In short, Christian attitudes toward Islam were not altogether different from American attitudes toward Nazis and Communists during the period 1937-85.

And who is to say that the Crusades, by hammering at the heartland of Islam, were not the reason for its ultimate containment? The First Crusade (1095-1101), which resulted in the recapture of Jerusalem, enabled Christians to occupy the Holy City for nearly a hundred years. Surrounding areas were held for another century or more, and agreements were reached which secured the rights of western pilgrims.

To boot, many of the side effects were positive. Technological skills and martial prowess were acquired in contests staged at a safe distance from home. Lisbon was reclaimed from Islam, while Catharism, a southern French heresy which held the institution of marriage in contempt and looked with favor on suicide, was defeated. Christianity entered Russia and Pomerania, and many souls were reconciled to the faith. Furthermore, while Eastern Orthodox leaders may have been embittered by the sack of Constantinople, this was not true in every instance. Some who had left the Catholic fold returned to it in a spirit of gratitude for western help against Muslim aggression.

Particulars aside, the popular image of the Crusades has given religion in general, and Catholicism in particular, a reputation for bellicosity that is hardly warranted. The most Catholic continent, South America, has been peaceful by comparison with Europe, Africa, and Asia. Few lives were lost in the Guatemalan civil war of 1954 — so few, in fact, that North American commentators concluded, on the basis of their own bloody record in 1861-65, that Guatemalans were politically indifferent. The truth is that they, and later their neighbors in Nicaragua, refrained from the kind of internecine killing, purges, and reprisals urged on them by U. S. advisers because it ran against the grain of their temperament and culture.[113] Equally inexplicable by Washington's standards was the behavior of Corazon Aquino, American-educated president of the

---

[113] On Nicaragua, see Violeta Barrios de Chamorro, *Dreams of the Heart* (1996), 274-77, 279, 285-86, 289, 295, 299-300, 305, 313, 324-25. On Guatemala, see Frederick W. Marks, "The CIA and Castillo Armas in Guatemala, 1954," *Diplomatic History* (Winter 1990), p. 84; also *Wall Street Journal*, December 30, 1996, p. 1. While it is true that Spain fought an ugly civil war (1936-39), most Spaniards had ceased to be Catholic in anything but name by 1930 (Warren Carroll, *The Last Crusade*, 8).

Philippines, who, during the 1980s, tolerated repeated coup attempts against her regime without apprehending those responsible and trying them on charges of treason.

The Inquisition

The age-old question of disloyalty and how a sovereign goes about dealing with it was the crux of the issue for court officials and churchmen at the time of the Spanish Inquisition. Did Spain persecute non-believers and resort to cruel and unusual punishment? At first sight, the answer appears to be "yes." But the closer one looks, the more one realizes that historical context, once again, has a critical bearing.

Curiously enough, the Inquisition had little to do with non-believers and everything to do with "fifth column" Catholics — individuals suspected of harboring Jewish or Moslem sympathies and consequently of trying to undermine Church and state from within. Its purpose was to rid Spain of subversives, not Muslims or Jews. Isabella's own confessor, along with the husband of her best friend, were of Jewish descent; and when Granada, the last redoubt of Moorish resistance, fell to the armies of the "Reconquista," Isabella granted her vanquished opponents full freedom of worship. They could have all the mosques they wanted. Such tolerance stands in striking contrast to the rule of Islam, which, then and now, refuses Christians similar rights.

Actually, the Inquisition had less to do with Catholicism than with Spain. There was nothing comparable in France, Austria, or Eastern Europe, and for reasons that are readily apparent. The Iberian peninsula, unlike other areas, was just emerging from a centuries-old civil war. It was honeycombed with Muslims and Jews whose ancestors had held sway since the eighth century when the forces of Islam, in league with the Jews, drove Christian defenders into mountain fastnesses. As Christians gradually reestablished themselves, large numbers of Muslims and Jews "converted" in order to retain their political and social standing, and not a few among them proceeded to undermine the new regime from within, viewing Muslim victories in other parts of the world as a cause for rejoicing. Not until 1571, when the Battle of Lepanto broke the naval power of Islam, did tension begin to wane. Americans during World War II, with far less cause for anxiety than Isabella's Spaniards, stripped Japanese-American nationals of their constitutional rights and consigned them to concentration camps.

Regarding methods of torture and execution, the comparative approach continues to shed light. In Geneva, Calvin burned Michael Servetus at the stake for denying the doctrine of the Trinity. Meanwhile, the French were boiling their victims alive, and in England, convicts were drawn and quartered after having their stomach cut out. When Henry VIII dispatched a group of Carthusian monks for refusing to recognize him as head of the English Church, his hangman cut out each man's heart and bowels. Then, after being burned at the stake, as well as beheaded and quartered, their remains were exhibited in public places.

Under "Good Queen Bess," the slightest intimation of dissent, political or religious, was put down with a sternness that would have shocked Spanish inquisitors.[114] Margaret Clitherow of York was crushed to death between huge slabs of stone for allowing Mass to be offered in her home. Archbishop O'Hurley of Cashel, Ireland, suffered yet another grisly fate. He was fitted with oil-filled iron boots which were heated to such a temperature that the flesh of his legs literally melted off his bones.

Considering that Catholics were wrapped in suits of straw to be set afire by the Japanese and slaughtered wholesale by the Turks at Otranto, Spanish reprisals were relatively mild. Both the Moriscos of Spain and Huguenots of France prior to St. Bartholomew's Day fell upon "papists" with incredible ferocity.

Only two thousand or 2% of those tried for treason by the Spanish were actually executed. The process was so fair, in fact, and prison conditions so tolerable under Torquemada (who has been roundly caricatured by English historians) that defendants accused of other crimes begged to have their cases brought before the Inquisition.

Miscarriages of justice were not unknown. But the Church mustered up sufficient courage to protest on occasion. Moreover, its stance in general was more lenient than that of the crown. When Isabella expelled the Jews from Spain, they found a safe haven in Rome, and Alexander VI, who was pope at the time, went a step

---

[114] Walsh, *Philip II*, 296.

further, prevailing on Naples and Venice to offer additional shelter. Nor did the Inquisition stifle cultural life, as has been alleged. On the contrary, it ushered in a golden age of art, science, and exploration. Iberia after Torquemada was a happier and safer place in which to live. While other nations were burning witches by the thousands, Spain remained self-possessed, and for the most part, tranquil.

Isabella expelled the Jews because the harmony that once existed between Jewish and Christian communities had broken down despite royal efforts to mediate. There had been massacres in Valladolid (1470), Cordoba (1474), and Seville (1478). In 1480, the Cortes of Toledo went so far as to separate Jewish and Christian neighborhoods. Isabella denounced violence against the Jews even as she tried to protect them by the issuance of decrees and letters. She contributed to the restoration of their synagogue in Gerona and forbade the levying of special taxes on their property. Several members of her court were Jewish, along with a trusted physician. Her personal secretary and almost all of her privy counselors were of Jewish descent.

Jews were not only perceived as undermining the state religion (for which there was a death penalty) but also as being contemptuous of Gentiles. It is from this period that the epithet "Christian dog" ("perro Cristiano") is said to date. Although they were far from numerous — only 25,000 families in all — their lockhold on trade and money-lending tended to fan the flames of fear and resentment. In Aragon, they charged 20% for a loan, in Castille 33%, and in Cuenca during the famine of 1376 they refused to lend for sowing at less than 40%.

Nor should the larger picture be overlooked. Jews were universally regarded as "foreigners." Spain was one of the few Christian countries where they were allowed to reside, and this by virtue of a special royal indult. England and France had already expelled them (in 1290 and 1306 respectively) and Bohemia would do so in 1542. Thus when Isabel issued her expulsion order in 1492, it was with the hearty approval of the English and French monarchs.

In sum, one's opinion of both the Inquisition and the Crusades will vary depending on whether one views them through modern lenses or the lenses of the time. And the same may be said in the case of Galileo.

Galileo

Religion mattered in 1620. Francis Bacon and other Protestants were as anxious as any Catholic to have Galileo silenced. Earlier, Copernicus won a respectful, if reserved, hearing from Rome for his theory of heliocentrism, which hypothesized what Galileo would later state as a fact. But the Pole was castigated by Luther. Similarly, Kepler, a Protestant, was condemned by the Protestant theological faculty of Tübingen for saying what Galileo would say ten years later. A similar fate befell the Jewish philosopher Spinoza, who was excommunicated and cursed by officials of his Dutch synagogue for airing ideas regarded as contrary to scripture. According to seventeenth century reports, the Jewish community actually tried to kill him.[115]

Galileo was never tortured, imprisoned, or excommunicated. Instead, he was placed under house arrest, and through it all, he lived in relative ease, receiving a wide circle of friends and colleagues including Milton and Hobbes. He continued to write, just as he continued to pursue his studies, on a generous church pension.

Did the Church err on a matter of faith and morals involving papal infallibility? No, because the Holy Father never took a formal position on heliocentrism. Even if he had, his teaching would have been more in the realm of science than theology and, as such, unprotected by his special faculty of infallibility. Furthermore, Galileo was not censured for *what* he taught so much as for *how* he taught it — that is, as fact instead of hypothesis, which is all it was at the time. By appearing to say, "The Bible is wrong" and doing so in a provocative manner, he shook the foundations of religion, and therefore of the state, in an era when politics and religion were closely linked. Not only was Galileo teaching something as fact that would remain unproven until 1835; but in holding that planets orbit the sun in perfect circles he was contradicting the findings of Kepler and Jesuit astronomers which were later proven correct. At the same time, he attacked a Jesuit over the nature of comets, holding — falsely again — that they were exhalations of the atmosphere.

---

[115] Steven Katz, ed., *Jewish Philosophers*, 138.

There is, finally, the issue of character. When Galileo learned of the invention of the telescope in Holland, he promptly built one of his own and proceeded to take full credit. Likewise, at his second trial for teaching heliocentrism as fact, he lied about the publication of an important work. Here, in short, was a man to whom truth was anything but sacrosanct. The antithesis of tact, he enjoyed putting his rivals to shame; and hence his sobriquet, "The Wrangler." Had he been a man of humbler mien, he would probably have avoided a brush with Church authority. But throughout his life, Galileo was a polemicist who delighted in the use of sarcasm, ridicule, and mockery to discomfit his adversaries.

The Church and the Holocaust

Another ecclesiastical judgment call that has attracted attention in recent years relates to papal policy during the Nazi Holocaust. Instead of charging ecclesiastical overreaction, however, adversaries view the Church in this case as unpardonably passive. Simply stated, Pope Pius XII is said to have done too little to save victims of the Hitler juggernaut. Rolf Hochhuth's play *The Deputy* (1963) and writings of similar bent hold that many lives could have been saved if only the Holy Father had spoken out more forcefully.

What one finds, however, is that the Vatican spoke very forcefully and that its protest went considerably beyond words.[116] What is remarkable is that Pius went as far as he did in view of the threat posed by Russian atheism.

Again, one must search out the facts. Pius XI's encyclical, *Mit Brennender Sorge* ("With Burning Anxiety"), which condemned Nazi ideology as neopagan in 1937, was written by Eugenio Pacelli, soon to be Pius XII; and when Pacelli assumed the papal office, his first encyclical, *Summi Pontificatus* (1939) echoed the theme of *Mit Brennender Sorge*. So stinging was its indictment that Hitler moved immediately to halt distribution.

In the Netherlands, a country where Catholic leaders reacted with unmitigated boldness against the Third Reich and its racial

---

[116] Most of the data and nearly all the quotes in the following section come from Anne Carroll's *Christ the King: Lord of History* (1985), 442-44.

policy, the results were tragic. Edith Stein was a Jewish convert to Catholicism who chanced to be stationed there as a nun, and it was partially in response to her insistence that the Church voice its opposition to Hitler in no uncertain terms that the Dutch Church took a clear and unequivocal stand. As a consequence, the Gestapo rounded up all Jewish Catholics, including Stein, and shipped them off to concentration camps, many of them never to return. Stein herself was put to death while Jewish Protestants were passed over.

News of the Dutch persecution reached Pius just as his own protest was about to appear in *Osservatore Romano*, the official Vatican newspaper — it was due that very evening. Incredulous at the Nazi reaction in Holland, he ordered his draft burned, saying, "If the protest of the Dutch bishops has cost the lives of 40,000 people, my intervention would take at least 200,000 people to their deaths."[117]

In his Christmas Message of 1942, Pius condemned persecution based on race, and in April 1943, he issued a message to the Slovak government objecting specifically to the persecution of Jews. When Berlin ordered Budapest to round up Hungarian Jews in April 1944, he protested with such vehemence that Hungarian officials refused to carry out the directive.

As Anne Carroll has observed, "the Pope did far more than issue statements. When Adolf Eichmann ordered a death march of 20,000 Jews from Budapest to Theresienstadt for extermination, Cardinal Seredi and the Papal Nuncio organized relief vehicles to accompany marchers with food and medicine. They carried several thousand blank papal conduct passes and rescued about 2,000 Jews. The nuncio personally hid 200 Jews in his palace." Caroll goes on to recall that,

> Pius XII instructed churches, monasteries and convents in Rome to take in Jews … Altogether, 55 monasteries and 100 convents in Rome were hiding Jews. Many Jews found refuge in the Vatican itself, including Dr. Zolli, the Chief Rabbi of Rome, who became a Catholic after the war. The Pope sent letters by hand to Italian bishops calling upon them to hide and rescue Jews.

---

[117] See *Il Seitimanale*, March 1, 1975, p. 40.

One of the main cities where this was done was Assisi, where the Franciscans coordinated hiding of Jews disguised as religious in cloisters, and printed false identity papers for them enabling them to escape past the American lines. In Italy, in fact, the majority of Jews were saved. The Pope also set up Delassem, an organization for assistance to foreign Jews. Four thousand received aid from this organization.[118]

All along, Vatican Radio and *Osservatore Romano* were informing the world of Nazi atrocities in Poland.

Jeno Levai, a Jewish historian and authority on the Holocaust, has shown that the pope did not remain silent when he could have saved lives; and Levai is backed by Pinchas E. Lapide, former Israeli consul in Italy, who concludes that "the Catholic Church saved more Jewish lives during the war than all the other churches, religious institutions and rescue organizations put together. Its record stands in startling contrast to the achievements of the International Red Cross and the Western Democracies."[119] In accordance with estimates of the postwar government of Israel that Pius saved 800,000 lives, a commemorative forest of as many trees was planted southeast of Jerusalem, and some years later, it was shown with ceremonial etiquette to Pope Paul VI in his first state visit to Israel.

Many are aware that Hitler was Catholic by birth. Fewer are conscious of the fact that he became an apostate, just as Stalin left Russian Orthodoxy. As an adult, Hitler was diametrically opposed to Catholic moral teaching; indeed, in the election that brought him to power, Catholic areas of Germany were among the few in which he lost.[120] Coincidentally, too, it was a Catholic officer, Count Claus Schenk von Stauffenberg, who made the first attempt on the Fuehrer's life.[121]

---

[118] Carroll, *Christ the King, Lord of History*, 444.

[119] Ibid.

[120] See Richard Hamilton, *Who Voted for Hitler* (Princeton University Press, 1982), 38-41, 371, 382.

[121] Portions of this section not drawn from Carroll's *Christ the King* come mainly from James Bogle, "The Real Story of Pius XII and the Jews" reprinted from the *Salisbury Review* by *Catalyst*, December 1996, pp. 8-11.

Chapter 4
Catholicism and Scripture

Suggestive as the foregoing may be, it is not by any means conclusive. We have covered much ground in a rather brief compass. But sooner or later, if we wish to identify Catholicism as the Church of Christ, we must demonstrate its conformity to specifications laid down by the Lord himself, citing chapter and verse. And so it is to this fundamental question that we now turn. Is Catholicism in harmony with the Bible? Can its sacraments, its practices in general, and particularly its teaching on controverted points such as priestly celibacy and marital indissolubility be defended on the basis of scripture?

Sola Scriptura

Such questions are all the more important given the animus of Protestant theologians against tradition as a basis for dogma and their concurrent unwillingness to rely on anything but scripture (*sola scriptura*). Ironically, when one searches for scriptural justification in support of a doctrine requiring such justification, it proves nonexistent. Nowhere in the Bible is scripture identified as the sole foundation of faith. On the contrary. Paul urges his Thessalonians to "hold fast to the traditions you were taught, whether by word or by epistle" (2 Thess. 2:15). While it is true that he and his colleagues quoted from the Old Testament, they also had recourse to tradition.[122]

---

[122] See, for example, 1 Cor. 10:4; 1 Peter 3:19; Jude 9. The case for tradition is further strengthened by Paul's charge to Timothy; "What you have heard from me through many witnesses entrust to faithful people who will have the ability to teach others" (2 Tim. 2:2).

Jesus himself never committed any of his thoughts to writing, so far as we know, but he did offer his apostles the assurance that "whoever *hears* you *hears* me" (Lk. 10:16 — italics added).

Sola scriptura is doubly hard to justify given that the New Testament, as we know it, did not exist for several hundred years after Pentecost. Not until late in the fourth century did a consensus emerge as to what should be included in its canon.[123] Thus it is the Church that gave us the Bible, rather than the other way around. Furthermore, even if there had been such a thing as a New Testament in the early years of evangelization, its impact on the average man would have been virtually nil, as he was unable to read.

Poverty and Celibacy

Supposing we assume, though, for the sake of argument that people in the days of St. Paul were literate and that the Bible was widely available in its present form. What would readers have discovered about the mind of the Master?

What kind of life, first of all, did Our Lord recommend to those whom he ordained to the ministry? They were to sell what they had and give alms, making for themselves "purses that do not grow old" (Lk. 12:33). They were also to prefer celibacy to marriage. In Christ's time, celibacy was regarded as a privilege reserved for scribes. Jesus' contribution was to open it to everyone. When Peter exclaimed, "Behold, we have left all and followed thee," the Master replied, "Amen I say to you, there is no one who has left house, or brothers, or sisters, or mother, or father or children, or lands, for my sake and for the gospel's sake who shall not receive now in the present time a hundredfold as much, houses and brothers, and sisters and mothers and children and lands."[124] And again, Jesus told his apostles, "There are eunuchs who were born so from their mother's womb, and there are eunuchs who were made so by men; and there are eunuchs who have made themselves so for the

---

[123] The canon of the Christian Bible was formulated at councils in Rome (382), Hippo (393), and Carthage (397). It was then submitted for approval to the bishop of Rome.

[124] Mk. 10:28-30; Mt. 19:29.

sake of the kingdom of heaven. Let him accept it who can" (Mt. 19:12). St. Paul, who voiced a similar preference, was himself celebrate, as was John the Baptist.[125] It goes without saying that Catholic religious orders are uniquely pledged to poverty and that celibacy is the rule for nuns and most priests.

The consecrated single life opens up a world of possibilities. During the years when American Catholics were relatively poor as a group and correspondingly rich in vocations to the religious life, their schools and health-care facilities were staffed by a corps of highly dedicated individuals willing to work for little more than bare subsistence. This, in turn, afforded low-income families quality education and nursing care at nominal fees. In many parts of the Third World, parents of underprivileged children, Protestant and Catholic alike, still regard their child's admission to a Catholic school as a dream come true.

In a larger sense, celibacy enables men and women to embark upon courses that might be judged rash, or at least imprudent, on the part of someone with a family to support. A recent survey found that half of all Protestant ministers would not enter the ministry if they had to do over again, and the reason most often given was stress on spouse and offspring.[126]

Critics like to picture the consecrated single life as "stifling," "repressive," and "unnatural," even ominous in terms of demographics. They paint it as a barrier to religious vocations, as well as a handicap for priests involved in marriage counseling. Then, as a trump card, they point out that priests and bishops of the generation after Christ were married.

In response to each of these objections, the Church has an answer. To begin with, it can be shown that Protestant seminaries, from the 1960s on, suffered as sharp a drop-off as their Catholic counterparts in the number of male applicants. Episcopal's General Theological Seminary in Chelsea (NYC), for example, had 75% fewer men in 1992 than it did in 1962 (*New York Times*, 7/20/92, p. B2 and 8/30/92, p. 34). Secondly, it makes no sense to assume that one has to be married in order to advise married couples. Must one be a woman

---

[125] 1 Cor. 7:8-9, 32-35, 38. See, in addition, for Jesus' view, Lk. 18:29.
[126] David Currie, *Born Fundamentalist, Reborn Catholic* (1996), 161.

to succeed as an OB-GYN? Are female psychiatrists the only ones qualified to treat women? Thirdly, many things recommended by Our Lord were "unnatural" in the sense of being "out of the ordinary" — fasting for one, love of one's enemies for another. The Christian learns to curb his appetites for the sake of a higher goal.

Jesus, Paul, and John the Baptist are prime examples of celibate genius in action. So, too, in the case of Plato, Michelangelo, Leonardo, Pascal, and Sir Isaac Newton, not to mention Corelli, Vivaldi, Handel, Beethoven, Schubert, and Brahms. Painters like Sir Joshua Reynolds, Thomas Cole, and Winslow Homer grace the list, as do the writers Jonathan Swift, Alexander Pope, Jane Austen, and Emily Brontë (Charlotte was single during the composition of *Jane Eyre*). When one adds the names of Washington Irving, Emily Dickinson, Louisa May Alcott, and Henry James, it hardly seems logical to view celibacy as a handicap. There was nothing stultified about Mother Teresa of Calcutta or the indefatigable pope who supported her.

Although we know from scripture, as well as tradition, that Peter was married, it is safe to say that he was a widower at the time of Christ's call. He is said to have been older than the other apostles, and it is his mother-in-law, rather than his wife, who is mentioned. None of the other apostles give any evidence of having been married. Although various women assisted Jesus in his ministry, none of them were wives of apostles. As Pope John Paul II declared in his general audience of July 17, 1993, "It appears that the twelve ... renounced family life in order to follow him."[127]

Admittedly, Christian clergymen of the second generation were married. To command respect in a traditionalist, hierarchical society, one had to be older and hence, under normal conditions, married. When Paul made enough converts in a given locality to form a faith community, it behooved him to be flexible in his choice of leaders. At the same time, we know from the latest research in early Christian manuscripts that priests of the earliest centuries were expected to live with their spouses as brother and sister and, as such, to cease generating children.[128] While not celibate in name, they were expected to behave as if they were.

---

[127] *Homiletic and Pastoral Review*, April 1995, p. 19.

[128] Alfons Maria Cardinal Stickler, *The Case for Clerical Celibacy* (1993).

Later, with the passage of time and a corresponding rise in the number of candidates for ordination, celibacy became increasingly viable, and although not imposed by law in the West until the 12th century, it was a trend from early on. At a bishops conference in Carthage in 390 A.D., it was decided that "what the apostles taught [in this regard] and what antiquity itself observed, let us also continue."[129] Some were surprised when priests of the ancient Syro-Malabar rite decided to embrace celibacy after two centuries of experimentation with marriage. Essentially, though, this was a case of history repeating itself.

It is worth noting that most of what Jesus taught, celibacy included, has a basis in the Old Testament. When Moses was about to receive the Ten Commandments, he asked Jewish males to honor the occasion by staying away from their wives. David and his followers refrained from marital intercourse for three days before consuming the Loaves of Proposition, and similar abstinence was enjoined during the Maccabean rededication of the temple. Jewish priests were likewise expected to remain apart from their spouses while engaged in offering temple sacrifice. It goes without saying that Catholic priests are privileged to offer the Holy Sacrifice of the Mass every day of the year.

In an age preoccupied with the body, when social custom and family pressure are apt to stampede young people into premature contact with the opposite sex, some kind of counterbalance is needed if the physical element of marriage, along with the institution itself, is to maintain its integrity. Consecrated celibacy serves as a useful corrective.

The Eucharist

Like clerical celibacy, the Catholic doctrine of the Real Presence of Christ in the Eucharist is a frequent target, and again it is firmly grounded in scripture. The sixth chapter of the Gospel of John, foreshadowing the Last Supper, quotes Jesus as telling his followers, "Unless you eat the flesh of the Son of Man and drink his blood you shall not have life in you ... for my flesh is meat

---

[129] *Homiletic and Pastoral Review*, April 1995, p. 25.

indeed and my blood is drink." Many of his listeners were scandalized by what they heard, calling it a "hard saying." But he presented them with a choice: either accept his words at face value or go their way. And "many," John tells us, chose the latter.

Three things are clear. First, Jesus insisted that his words be taken literally. Secondly, his audience was aware of this. And thirdly, "many," not just a few, bolted. Our Lord would not have risked the loss of even one soul for want of clarification if he had been speaking figuratively because this was not his way. When Nicodemus was baffled by his use of the expression "born again," he explained (John 3). When he spoke of the difficulty a rich man might encounter gaining access to heaven and his apostles seemed at a loss, he developed the point (Mk. 10:26-27). A third time, when he warned about the leaven of the Pharisees and his disciples missed the point, he leveled with them (Mt. 16. See also John 11:13-14).

St. Paul spoke tellingly of the Eucharist when he described it as something so extraordinary that to receive it unworthily was to be "guilty of the body and blood of the Lord" and to eat and drink "judgment to oneself."[130]

Jesus' own words at the Last Supper were, "take and eat" for "this is my body ... this is my blood." He could easily have said, "this represents my body" or "this is a symbol of my body" or "think of me when you eat and drink together." Instead, his language was that of transubstantiation (the miraculous change by which ordinary bread and wine become the body and blood of Christ).[131]

Without question, the doctrine of the Real Presence requires faith. But if one were to eliminate every tenet of Christian teaching that rises above the level of the human intellect, there would be no Virgin Birth, no Incarnation, no miracles, and no Resurrection.

Isaiah had it right: God's ways are not man's ways. For thirty years, Jesus labored in silence behind the walls of a carpenter shop in a remote town of an outlying province. Why would God hide? Why would he call the poor "blessed" and enjoin his followers to love their enemies? Why would he urge his apostles to renounce

---

[130]   1 Cor. 11:27-29.
[131]   See, for a good discussion of the Church Fathers on this topic, Gibbons, *Faith of Our Fathers*, ch. 21.

family life and prepare for persecution? If he could change water into wine, raise men from the dead and walk away from his own tomb, is it too much to expect that he might have given himself physically under the appearance of bread and wine? Hard to believe, perhaps, but not unreasonable.

What could be more appropriate, actually, than that Jesus should come to us under forms of food and drink symbolic of warmth and well-being, for this is what the Eucharistic Sacrifice is all about. Bethlehem, the place of his birth, means "house of bread." He was laid in a manger where beasts of burden find sustenance, and he likened himself to a vine that nourishes its branches. In the parable of the prodigal son, a banquet is served; and when Our Lord calls Peter to shepherd his flock, he tells him to "feed my lambs." One notes that his command was not to "guide" or "watch over" them, but rather to "feed" them. Jesus multiplied loaves. He broke bread with his apostles at the Last Supper. He gave them breakfast on the shore of the Sea of Galilee following the Resurrection. And he directed Jairus to offer his risen daughter "something to eat" (Mk. 5:43).

Jesus' physicality is quite remarkable. It was not out of character for him to make a solution of mud paste with his saliva and apply it to a man's eyes (John 9). Not only did he embrace children, reach out to adults, and allow himself to be touched.[132] He also berated his host on one occasion for not giving the traditional kiss of welcome. And when a woman of dubious reputation went out of her way to anoint his feet with tears and dry them with her hair, he commended her. He even insisted on washing the feet of his apostles.

This Son of Man shed tears. He allowed his torturers to strip away his clothing and pound cold metal through his extremities. And after the Resurrection, he invited doubting Thomas to "put your hand into my side."

It is hard to imagine anything more physical than the matrimonial bonding of man and woman in "one flesh." Yet, this is the very image Jesus uses when he identifies himself as the "bridegroom" of the Church and offers himself in the Eucharist.[133] Occa-

---

[132] For example, Mk. 1:41 and Mt. 9:26, 29.
[133] For "bridegroom," see John 3:29.

sionally, one may hear it said in affectionate jest, "I'd like to eat you up!" Incredible as it may seem, this is precisely what Our Lord invites us to do in the most sublime of all mysteries.

One hastens to add that neither Christ's physicality nor the prevalence of feeding imagery in the gospels are sufficient, in and of themselves, to sustain a Catholic interpretation of Holy Communion. They must be viewed in conjunction with Christ's words and the conviction of the early Church. A letter written around 110 A.D. by Ignatius of Antioch and accepted by Protestants, as well as Catholics, calls the Eucharist "the flesh of our Savior." One can also cite Justin Martyr in the second century, Origen in the third, Chrysostom and Cyril of Jerusalem in the fourth, and Augustine in the fifth.[134]

Confession

It is hard to imagine that the sacrament of reconciliation whereby the priest assigns penance and grants absolution to a penitent on the basis of confession and a firm purpose of amendment would be a sore point with anyone familiar with the Bible. Jesus, who forgave sins verbally, conferred this power on his apostles when he told them, "Whose sins you shall forgive they are forgiven, and whose sins you shall retain, they are retained" (John 20:21-23). How can a priest know which sins to forgive, and on what terms, unless they are verbally confessed? In line with this, James urged his followers to "confess" their sins to one another.[135]

We also know from the *Didache*, mentioned earlier and one of the few authoritative sources for knowledge of life in the early Church (it was written before 100 A.D.), that Christians made it a practice to confess their sins every Sunday before Mass.

In short, there is a documentary basis not only for the sacrament of reconciliation but also for the importance traditionally attached to it by the Church. It was not by accident that Christ's public ministry began with the word "repent."[136] His very first or-

---

[134] Gibbons, *Faith of Our Fathers*, 243-44.

[135] James 5:16.

[136] Mk. 1:15.

der of business on entering the Upper Room where the apostles were gathered on Easter Sunday was repentance and remission of sin, just as this appears in his last instruction. It was a theme he never tired of driving home.[137]

Doubtless, it is easier and less embarrassing to confess one's sins directly to God; but direct confession lacks the element of vocal assurance, along with the moral support and counsel that a good confessor can afford. Secondly, pride, which is the root of all evil, is hard to overcome, and the sting of humiliation associated with owning up on one's knees can be as purifying to the soul as alcohol is to an open wound. Frequent confession is a special aid to married couples because it accustoms them to uttering words of apology, and if there is anything a loyal spouse needs to hear on occasion, in addition to the phrase, "I love you," it's "I'm sorry, dear."

Not only does confession sweep away misgivings and prepare the soul for a worthy reception of Holy Communion. It also forces the penitent to face up to his or her failings. Members of Alcoholics Anonymous are urged to admit their shortcomings publicly whenever it is opportune, and AA is the most successful of all support groups.

Psychiatrists have long recognized that the soul must be purged of guilt, and what better way than through penance? Many a child, caught in an act of wrongdoing, yearns inwardly for chastisement. Some go so far as to demand it. And there is an element of the child in all of us. Tykes appreciate hearing that they are forgiven, and so do we.

Some shy away from the sacrament of reconciliation because they fear the priest will echo Christ's words to the woman caught in adultery: "Go thy way and sin no more." Yet this is precisely what they need to hear. Others find themselves confessing the same sin over and over again because sin is by nature habitual, and habits are hard to shake. But even the most intractable habit will yield in time to the grace of the sacrament given a firm purpose of amendment. Just as radiation therapy for cancer requires patience, so too in the case of penance, which treats spiritual cancer.

---

[137] John 20:21-23 (upper room); Lk. 24:47 (last instruction). See also Mt. 11:20-24; 12:41; 21:32; Mk. 6:12-13; Lk. 18:10-14. For Paul, see Romans 2:4-5.

For the record, Catholics are not obliged to go to confession unless a priest is readily available. Nor is there any obligation to confess venial sins, only those that are "mortal"; and for a sin to be mortal — that is, grave — it must involve serious matter and be committed with full knowledge of its import, full deliberation, and full consent of the will. However, since venial sin, if allowed to go unchecked, can lead to more heinous offenses, it is prudent to engage the enemy at the outermost ramparts of one's spiritual citadel and receive grace at regular intervals. Just as an automobile requires periodic oil changes to lubricate its moving parts and maximize running performance, so, too, in the case of the soul. We need to have our "spiritual fluids" refreshed from time to time if we are to avoid a buildup of the kind of moral sludge that will eventually erode the joy of conscious integrity and hamper our relations with others.

Let it be said, in addition, that penitents are entitled to anonymity. No one is obliged to confess face-to-face or to a particular member of the clergy, and confessors are pledged to the strictest confidence. Priests have been known to give their lives rather than break the seal of the confessional. Centuries ago, in the city of Prague, a man of the cloth by the name of Nepomuk was executed by the king — thrown into the river and drowned — for refusing, as the queen's spiritual director, to divulge details of her confession.

The Papacy

Papal headship, the final feature of Catholicism under consideration in the present chapter, is a tenet whose importance cannot be overstated, for it is upon the teaching authority of the Magisterium that all other beliefs ultimately depend.

Few students of scripture would deny that Jesus set up a hierarchical organization. He gathered seventy-two "disciples" (Lk. 10:1) and selected twelve for intimate association. The "Twelve" joined him for the Last Supper and occupied a cardinal place in the power structure. At the same time, within this inner group there was one individual who towered above all the others, and his name was Peter.

Jesus conferred the power to forgive sins on the Twelve as a whole (John 20:19-23). However, it was to Peter alone that he entrusted the "keys" to the kingdom with authority to "bind" and "loose":

> Thou art Peter, and upon this rock I will build my Church, and the gates of hell shall not prevail against it. And I will give thee the keys of the kingdom of heaven; and whatever thou shalt bind on earth shall be bound in heaven, and whatever thou shalt loose on earth shall be loosed in heaven (Mt. 16:18-19).

When King Hezekiah turned over the keys to Eliakim, he was appointing him chief minister (Isaiah 22:20-22). And such was the case with Peter. Keys, in Christ's time, were a symbol of authority.

Peter was the only apostle instructed by Our Lord to "feed my lambs ... feed my sheep" (John 21:15-17), and as Christ's vicar, he came first on every official list of apostles.[138] He is the only one Christ is known to have singled out as a special object of prayer (Lk. 22:32), likewise the only one to have his name changed by Jesus — from Simon to Peter, meaning "rock." The change is significant as only a handful of individuals are so honored in the Old Testament. Abram's name was changed to Abraham, Sarai's to Sarah, and Jacob's to Israel.

Peter alone was entrusted with the task of "strengthening" his "brethren" (Lk. 22-31-32). He was also the first to identify Jesus as the Messiah (Mt. 16:16), as well as the first to enter the empty tomb (John 20:6). When our Lord made a point of asking Peter whether he loved him more than any of the other apostles, Peter replied in the affirmative (John 21:15).

Peter alone identifies himself in the gospels as a sinner (Lk. 5:8), and after the cock crows, he weeps tears of remorse. He is the first apostle to see the risen Christ, just as he alone among the apostles has the distinction of being called "blessed" by the Lord, recalling Gabriel's salutation to Mary (Mt. 16:17).[139]

---

[138] For example, Mt. 10:1-4; Mk. 3:16-19; Lk. 6:14-16; and Acts 1:13.
[139] Lk. 24:34; 1 Cor. 15:5.

In all the books of the Bible, there is only one individual whom God associates with himself by use of the pronoun "we" (Mt. 17:23-26). Peter alone among the apostolic band had his tax paid by Jesus (Mt. 17:26) and furnished the boat from which his master taught (Lk. 5:3). Hence the phrase "barque of Peter" in reference to the papacy. Almost always, when questions were directed to Jesus by the apostles, they came from Peter. And when queries traveled in the other direction, it was Peter who generally acted as spokesman for the group.

A fair amount of evidence for Peter's primacy postdates the Resurrection. At the Council of Jerusalem, when the question of requirements for Gentile conversion sparked heated discussion, it was he who intervened and restored calm (Acts 15:7 and 12). Similarly, after Jesus ascended into heaven and sent the Holy Spirit to strengthen his apostles at Pentecost, Peter decided on the method of choosing an apostle to replace Judas (Acts 1:15-26). Subsequently, he was the first to address the rulers of the Jews (Acts 4:8-9), the first to work a miracle, and the first to preach on behalf of the Church.[140] He was also the first to take Christianity to the Gentiles (Acts 10), the first to cure (Acts 3:1-10), and the only one of the Twelve to raise a person from the dead (Acts 9:36-43). Luke tells us that Peter's power over illness was such that the sick waited patiently for his shadow to fall upon them (Acts 5:12-16). Beyond this, he was the only one of the Twelve in whose presence a man and woman were struck dead for chicanery (Acts 5:1-11).

Peter was consulted on every vital issue in the early Church so that no decision of any moment was taken without his approval.[141] True it is that he was rebuked by Paul for backsliding on tactics regarding Gentile conversion (Gal. 2:11). But there is no reason to believe that such chiding undercut his authority. The Holy Father listens every day to disgruntled cardinals. Yet he remains *Il Papa*. And if the writings of Paul and others occupy more space in the New Testament than do those of Peter, this again is to be expected, for Peter was the administrator.

---

[140] Acts 2:14; 3:6-7.

[141] See, for instance, Acts 1:15-26; 5:29; 15:6-12; and John 21:1-11 (illustrating Peter's leadership).

Paul, after returning from Arabia following his conversion and spending three years in Damascus, went up to Jerusalem to the home of Peter, where he stayed fifteen days. He saw James, we are told, but none of the other apostles. And so here, as elsewhere, it is Peter who occupies center stage.[142]

When Paul was called upon to settle a dispute in Antioch over requirements for Gentile conversion, he took it "to the apostles and presbyters at Jerusalem" because this is where authority resided (Acts 15:1-5). In another passage, he distinguishes between himself and "men of authority" (Gal. 2:6). Such was never the case with Peter.

The first pope spoke with an air of authority unmatched by any other apostle. He is the only author of Sacred Scripture ever to pronounce judgment on the writing of a fellow author, warning that Paul's epistles can be confusing to those who are either unstable in the faith or lacking in erudition (2 Peter 3:16). Secondly, while making clear that "no prophecy is made by private interpretation," he exempts himself and uses the impersonal "we": "We have the word of prophecy ... to which you do well to attend" (2 Peter 1:19-20). This is the same Peter who presents the most extensive analysis in all of the New Testament on the anatomy of evil.[143]

While it is true that halfway through Acts, Christ's lead apostle "peters out" and the spotlight shifts to Paul, a fact not lost on Protestant commentators, the administrative pattern had, by this time, been set. Peter established himself at the epicenter from whence his associates could reach every part of the known world in response to Christ's injunction to "preach to all nations."[144]

---

[142] See Gal. 1:18.

[143] 2 Peter 2. Although the authorship of the second letter of Peter has been called into question, its attribution to Peter will suffice for our purposes. If the author was someone other than Peter, this "someone" was close enough to the lead apostle to speak on his behalf (see 2 Peter 1:1).

[144] For evidence that Peter was in Rome, see 1 Peter 5:13 (Rome was known as "Babylon" by the early Christians). Paul's epistle to the Romans, where he describes the faith of the Christian community in Rome as "spoken of throughout the whole world" and declares that he himself has not yet visited Rome, though he hopes to do so when he sets out later for Spain, is also pertinent

Protestant theologians inclined to grant Peter's authority will deny the existence of convincing evidence for a transfer of petrine power to succeeding pontiffs. But how likely is it that papal leadership of the type ordained by Jesus would have been denied by God to generations faced with mounting challenges of unity and command? If ever there was need for a man like Peter, it would have been in the post-Pentecostal age.[145]

History has shown that the papacy is the only institution capable of holding the main body of Christians together. Protestantism, without any sure ground of unity, has shattered into somewhere between twenty and thirty thousand sects, all claiming preferred status. At the time of Luther and Calvin, some rejected practices perceived as contrary to scripture, while others such as the Anabaptists would only subscribe to practices expressly endorsed by scripture. Within a few years of the Reformation, no fewer than a hundred meanings had been attached to the words, "This is my Body ... this is my Blood."[146]

Today, Protestant spokesmen disagree on everything from predestination to the Real Presence. Some condemn abortion; others find it acceptable. For every vote against remarriage after divorce, there are votes in its favor. Artificial birth control, euthanasia, and "gay marriage" all find a measure of acceptance among the leaders of our separated brethren. Indeed, there isn't a single doctrine taught by one Protestant church that is not denied by another, excepting perhaps the existence of God.

[144 cont.] (see Romans 1:8, 10-13; 15:22-24). Peter is known to have traveled with Mark the Evangelist, and he mentions Mark's presence in Rome (1 Peter 5:13). This is corroborated by Paul, writing at a later date from a Roman prison (Col. 4:10). See also Ignatius of Antioch's Epistle to the Romans 4:3 (110 A.D.). Ignatius writes: "Not as Peter and Paul did do I command you ... They were apostles and I am a convict." All the Church Fathers who touch on the point connect Peter with Rome, and none deny it (see *This Rock*, January 1997, pp. 30-32, for a listing of such Fathers and quotations from each.)

[145] Cardinal Newman, in *An Essay on the Development of Christian Doctrine* (New York edition, 1845), attributes the sparsity of reference to papal leadership during the first few centuries to a lack of need for such leadership (pp. 80-92). But, as he points out, when the need arose for a spiritual sheet anchor, it was in place.

[146] Gibbons, *Faith of Our Fathers*, 240.

Among Fundamentalists there are some who accept tobacco but forbid mixed swimming while others do the opposite. Only two out of five self-proclaimed evangelicals agree that Jesus was at once true man and true God.[147] "First-degree separationists" refuse to socialize with anyone outside their sect. Others go a step further. A "second-degree separationist" declines to associate even with people within his sect if *they* socialize outside. Some believe in segregating congregations along social and racial lines — Fundamentalist schools have been known to forbid interracial dating. Others find such practices revolting.[148]

In contrast to this veritable Babel of theological dissonance, the Catholic Church has spoken with remarkable consistency on matters of faith and morals for nearly two thousand years. So impervious has it been to tides of opinion that as recently as 1994 it was able to issue an 800-page catechism binding on all.

Jesus never prayed in vain, and one of the things He prayed for was "complete" unity among his followers (John 17:21-23). "There shall be one fold, one shepherd," he assured his listeners (John 10:16), and if a man refused to hear the Church, he should be treated "as the heathen" (Mt. 18:17). We have, in addition, Paul's pleas for unity (1 Cor. 1:10-12; 3:4; Eph. 4:3-5; Phil. 2:2) along with Peter's warning against lying teachers who would bring in "destructive sects" (2 Peter 2:1). Paul could hardly have been clearer in upholding the importance of doctrinal consistency: "Even if we or an angel from heaven should preach a gospel to you other than that which we have preached to you, let him be anathema!" (Gal. 1:8). Which Christian body in the present age corresponds most closely to this apostolic vision of unity?

In recent years, with more and more scholars inclined to question the reliability of Sacred Scripture, the Holy Father has responded with reassuring firmness. In 1964, the Pontifical Biblical Commission reaffirmed that what Jesus taught "was firmly impressed on the mind [of his listeners] and easily remembered" and that "there is no reason to doubt that the apostles passed on to their listeners what was really said and done by the Lord." The 1994 Catechism says essentially the same thing: "The Church holds

---

[147]   Currie, *Born Fundamentalist*, 166.

[148]   Ibid., 21, 197.

firmly that the four Gospels, 'whose historicity she unhesitatingly affirms, faithfully hand on what Jesus ... really did and taught'" (sec. 126). While it recognizes that the evangelists may have been selective in the recounting of events and that the gospels don't always follow strict chronological order, it nonetheless vouches for the reliability of all that they contain.[149]

History as Witness

Over and above the testimony of scripture and the need for a central ground of unity, there is a third plank in the Church's case for petrine succession, and it derives from the history of early Christianity.

When dissension broke out in the church of Corinth around 95 A.D., Pope Clement sent a letter to the Corinthians that rang with authority, as well as moderation. Whether or not his opinion was requested, it was heeded, and his words were read for centuries. There is also the testimony of St. Ignatius, Bishop of Antioch (Peter's see after he left Jerusalem) from 69 to 107 A.D. In Ignatius' words, the Roman Church "presides over the whole assembly united in charity," and he asks prayers for the flock confided to him subject to Christ and the supreme authority of Rome.[150] A third voice giving witness down through the centuries to papal primacy is that of St. Irenaeus of Lyons (c. 125-203). Irenaeus, who defended brilliantly against heresy, stated on one occasion that "all churches ... must ... be in harmony with this church [Rome] on account of its lofty preeminence. In her Christians of every land have preserved the apostolic tradition."[151]

Around the time of Irenaeus, a question arose as to the proper day for celebrating Easter. In the East, it was Passover; but for the

---

[149] Much the same language is to be found in Vatican Council II's *Dei Verbum*. See Frederick Marks, "The Reliability of the Bible," *Homiletic and Pastoral Review* (December 1998), pp. 25-30.

[150] Rumble and Carty, *Radio Replies*, III, 85.

[151] Irenaeus, *Against Heresies*, 3, 3, 2. Harnack, the German Protestant scholar, accepted Clement's letter as proof that the primacy of the bishop of Rome was taken for granted as early as the first century (see Rumble and Carty, *Radio Replies*, III, 85).

West it fell on the first Sunday after the full moon of the vernal equinox. Pope Victor (189-98), opting for western custom, ordered recalcitrant bishops into line; and by the beginning of the third century, Roman practice was the norm.[152]

Papal supremacy was accepted by every Church Father, including those whose orthodoxy is recognized by Protestants: Augustine, Jerome, Ambrose, Basil, Chrysostom, and Cyprian. With one voice, they all paid homage to the bishop of Rome as their spiritual head. In the words of Ambrose, "Where Peter is, there is the Church." Augustine, for his part, summed it up as well as anyone when he wrote that "the acts of two councils were sent to the Apostolic See whence an answer was returned. The question is closed."[153]

Rome and Orthodoxy

Of all the proofs for papal infallibility, none, perhaps, is more striking than the sheer consistency of Catholic teaching over a span of 2,000 years. With the exception of a handful of "bad" popes, whose personal lives left something to be desired, and a predictable number of weak administrators, the papacy has been well served. But no pope, good, bad, or indifferent, has ever taught anything in the realm of faith or morals that had to be retracted by a successor. Even during the high tide of the Arian heresy, when all eastern dioceses and most in the West were headed by dissident bishops, Rome hewed to the truth. Likewise in the area of matrimonial law, groups of bishops have bowed to pressure for the granting of unwarranted annulments. The Roman pontiff never. No other institution in history can lay claim to such a record.

Popes have been imprisoned and tortured. But none has ever surrendered on faith and morals. Dozens chose martyrdom over apostasy, and many have been declared saints. One, Lucius II, was murdered for standing up to the Roman mob. Liberius, whose tenure dates to the fourth century, was imprisoned for two years, threatened with execution, and cruelly treated by those who hoped to

---

[152] Henri Daniel Rops, *The Church of Apostles and Martyrs* (1962), I, 388n; Gibbons, *Faith of Our Fathers*, 91.

[153] Gibbons, *Faith of Our Fathers*, 107 (for Augustine).

procure a heretical statement from him. Yet such a statement was not forthcoming.

It was the same with the sixth century pope, Vigilius. A heretic before becoming pope, he owed his accession to the baleful influence of Theodora, wife of the emperor, who expected him to continue in office as a heretic. But once he occupied the chair of Peter, his views changed. "Formerly," he wrote, "I spoke wrongly and foolishly. Though unworthy, I am Vicar of Blessed Peter." Vigilius' about-face cost him ten years of white martyrdom ending in a painful and ignominious death.[154]

In marked contrast to the papal record, theologians by the hundreds, if not thousands, have ranged themselves on the side of error. It was they, not the Holy Father, who argued for a monarch's right to enslave the natives of the New World, and they who favored the death penalty for heresy.[155] Many of them took up the cudgels for conciliarism, which at one time was practically a badge of academic respectability, the idea being that decisions taken by a church council take precedence over the ruling of a pope.[156] Not a few, including Martin Luther, as mentioned earlier, supported bigamy.[157] And when Henry VIII petitioned Rome for permission to marry Anne Boleyn, he was supported by all the leading lights of Cambridge as well as by every bishop in the land save one.

This is not to suggest that every pontiff has been brilliant or administratively clever. While Paul IV (1555-59) knew most of the Bible by heart, Eugenius III (1145-53) was unlearned, timid, and naive.[158] There could scarcely have been a less auspicious choice on the part of the College of Cardinals. Yet once installed, Eugenius functioned rather well.

---

[154] For Liberius and Vigilius, see Carroll, *The Building of Christendom*, 31-33, 168, 172-78. For Vigilius, see Currie, *Born Fundamentalist*, 94-96.

[155] *Catholic Evidence Training Outlines*, 74; *Our Sunday Visitor*, August 9, 1992, p. 6.

[156] Warren Carroll, *The Glory of Christendom*, 471.

[157] On Old Testament grounds, see the *New Catholic Encyclopedia* article on Luther.

[158] Walsh, *Philip II*, 173-74 (on Paul IV).

Popes have resigned, and one of them designated his own successor.[159] There have likewise been intervals lasting years between papal reigns when Rome cruised on auto-control (e.g., 1292-94).

Plainly, the human element has been subsumed by something greater. To come to any other conclusion would be to overlook the frequency with which papal authority has been tested, along with the type of power brought to bear by it enemies. We are speaking here not only of dissident theologians and ad hoc councils.[160] Cardinals have formed cabals and elected anti-popes to do their bidding, while kings and emperors have wielded the weapons of state.[161]

Rome Against the World

Byzantine potentates challenged Rome on the issues of monotheism and iconoclasm between the 7th and 9th centuries, and they were no mean opponents. Yet not a single one prevailed.

During the 800s, Pope Nicholas would not permit Lothair II of France to discharge his rightful wife, Theutberga, in favor of a mistress. Lothair went ahead, however, securing the backing of two powerful archbishops and persuading a church synod to act as a rubber-stamp. Nicholas, equally determined, preferred captivity in St. Peter's without food to surrendering on a matter of principle, and in the end, after deposing Lothair's bishops, it was he who emerged victorious.[162]

Two centuries later, Gregory VII (Hildebrand) took on Henry IV of Germany in a political contest that resulted in Henry's coming barefoot as a penitent to the papal suite at Canossa.[163]

---

[159] Felix III (526-30) designated his own successor (see Carroll, *The Glory of Christendom*, 37). Gregory VI resigned in 1046; and Celestine V (1294) resigned after several months owing to a sense of personal inadequacy.

[160] Carroll, *The Glory of Christendom*, 502 (for an example of conciliar opposition).

[161] Ibid., 396-97.

[162] See John Farrow, *The Pageant of the Popes*, 77-78.

[163] After his dramatic act of submission at Canossa, Henry again turned on Gregory; but the pontiff never relented in his battle against government interference in religious affairs. After a life dedicated to the stamping out of simony and clerical philandering, Gregory was constrained to flee Rome to avoid capture by Henry's armies. "I have loved justice and hated wickedness," he remarked, "therefore I die in exile."

By 1100, the eastern and western emperors were so angry with the Roman pontiff that they refused to have any further dealings with him. Eventually, though, it was Emperor Frederick Barbarosa who bent the knee, travelling to Rome as a suppliant.[164]

During the same period, Pope Alexander III crossed swords with Henry II of England over an issue involving Thomas à Becket, Archbishop of Canterbury. Thomas stood in the way of Henry's attempt to abolish clerical immunity from prosecution in secular courts, and for this he was struck down on the high altar by four knights acting with Henry's tacit approval. Nevertheless, it was Henry who yielded. As Warren Carroll puts it, Henry ended his reign,

> condemned by all Christendom, ordered by the Pope on Holy Thursday 1171 not to enter any church, fleeing vainly to Ireland to try to escape the loathing he felt all around him, reconciled with the Church more than a year later at the price of giving up all he had taken from and contended for against Becket, compelled finally (not by the Pope, but by the sheer force of public opinion) to walk to Canterbury in the summer of 1174, barefoot in the rain, wearing a hair shirt such as was found on Becket's body after his murder, kissing the pillar where Thomas was struck down, kneeling at his tomb and giving money so that lamps might forever burn there, having himself publicly whipped by several bishops, an abbot, and eighty monks.[165]

To the above list of clashes between papal and royal authority may be added the following: Urban II vs. Philip I of France (Urban excommunicated Philip for abandoning his wife and "marrying" the wife of another man); Innocent III vs. Count Raymond of Toulouse; Celestine II (and Innocent III) vs. Philip II. Celestine overruled an annulment granted at the local level which would have permitted Philip to forsake his wife, the Danish princess Ingeborg. Innocent, on assuming office, backed his predecessor, placing all of France

---

[164] In this case, Alexander was fortunate to have the support of the French under Louis VII. See Caroll, *Glory of Christendom*, 114, 116.

[165] Ibid., 107-108. Needless to say, today's courts prosecute clerics for infractions of the law as a matter of course.

under papal interdict for thirteen years until Philip, one of the most powerful of French rulers, consented to take Ingeborg back. Pope Gregory IX challenged Frederick II, and during the 16th century, Clement VII set aside the demands of Henry VIII of England.[166]

In recent times, Pius VI resisted efforts on the part of French radicals under Danton, Robespierre, and Napoleon to take over the Church. He was pursued by French armies and finally captured. But neither Pius, who died in captivity, nor his successor would give way. After Pius VII rejected Napoleon's appeal for an annulment of his brother's marriage to Miss Patterson of Baltimore, Napoleon ceased consulting the Holy See.[167] Like his predecessor of the same name, Pius was taken prisoner by the French and threatened. But Bonaparte's fate was sealed. Never again would he triumph on the field of battle; and in the end, it was he, rather than the Holy Father, who stood behind bars.

To recapitulate, the papacy has an absolutely unique track record. Unlike the Eastern Orthodox patriarchs of Turkey and Russia, who were routinely subservient to the will of Constantinople and Moscow, unlike Anglican, Lutheran, and Presbyterian leaders whose behavior was governed by the union of church and state, Peter's successors have clung tenaciously, and for the most part successfully, to their moral imperium. Once, when the Holy Father appeared headed for vassal status as a resident of Avignon, Catherine of Siena persuaded him to leave France and return to Rome, where his capacity for independent judgment would be unassailable.

Christ promised to build his church on solid ground, and so he did. When he said, "Thou are Peter and upon this rock I shall build my church, and the gates of hell will not prevail against it," when he assured his followers that the Holy Spirit would dwell with them "forever" and teach them "all the truth," he was outlining the shape of the future.[168]

We may not have first-hand knowledge of the Risen Lord, as did the apostles. But we are in the presence of something equally telling, a record of continuity in ecclesiastical teaching that stretches over two thousand years and defies all natural explanation. If there

---

[166] Ibid., 216, 229.
[167] Gibbons, *Faith of Our Fathers*, 339.
[168] John 14:16-17; 16:12-13.

is servility in accepting papal judgment on matters of faith and morals, as is often charged, then it is the servility of a prince pledging fealty to a king who has never defaulted. No pope has ever staked out a position on faith and morals that is not eminently defensible from a purely rational standpoint.

Has Church Teaching Changed?

According to certain critics, there have been changes in Church teaching over the years. Catholics are no longer obliged to abstain from meat on Friday provided they practice mortification in keeping with the spirit of the day on which Christ died. Similarly, non-Catholic parties to mixed marriages are no longer required to promise in writing that their offspring will be raised in the faith. Usury is no longer singled out for condemnation; slavery is. Married men may become priests in Eastern Europe, but not in the West.

At first sight, Catholic teaching appears to be little more than a function of time and place. But further investigation uncovers no evidence that there has been any shift whatever in the body of doctrine known as "dogma." The Decalogue is still in place. So, too, the admonitions of Christ's Sermon on the Mount. Clearly, the challenge here is to distinguish between what is, and is not, subject to change. May a boy of thirteen, who has gone to work to support disabled parents, dispense with filial respect and obedience simply because he is installed as breadwinner? No. And so it is with Church teaching, which remains constant in the realm of faith and morals while adapting when it comes to custom, style, and discipline.

The Ten Commandments, though handed down to a particular people at a particular time, were intended as benchmarks for all people of all time. And the same applies to what Jesus and his vicars have to say on poverty, celibacy, and divorce; similarly, when it comes to abortion, contraception, suicide, and sodomy, along with doctrines such as the divinity of Christ, the real presence of Jesus in the Eucharist, and papal infallibility. Church teaching on faith and morals is immutable.

During the 1960s, when the Divine Liturgy underwent radical change, Catholicism seemed to be in a state of flux. However, it was externals, rather than the essence of the faith, that changed. Liturgy and dogma may overlap, but they are not synonymous.

Guidelines on modesty are another case in point. For centuries, women in remote parts of the world went about scantily clad, and it may not have been sinful or scandalous in light of local custom. Even in the industrialized West, hemlines and necklines have been known to rise and fall with startling rapidity. In such cases, church teaching is at once rigid and flexible — rigid in the sense of promoting chastity, yet flexible in recognizing the role of fashion.

Usury, Torture, and Slavery

Usury comes under the same heading as dress, since it is largely a function of circumstance. Economic and legal changes over the centuries have transformed the nature of money and money lending to such a degree that the charging of interest on a loan (usury in its original sense) is rarely unjust, unconscionable, or gravely damaging.

In the case of torture, history has worked in reverse, making current practice in certain areas seem more, rather than less, objectionable. People of the present age have a much lower tolerance for pain. They are more cerebral, less hardy physically (while, at the same time, more carnal), and heavily dependent upon anesthesia and other pain killers, not to mention thermostatic heat and air conditioning. Again, the root issue is ethical, as opposed to moral, because there is nothing inherently wrong with punishment. The question is not so much *whether* to punish as *how* to do so and to what degree. The day may come when it will be unethical for an entrepreneur to dismiss employees without proof of negligence. Many a family man with his back to the wall would prefer twenty lashes to the scourge of long-term unemployment. Should such a day dawn and the weight of collective conscience come down on the side of workers' rights, the church would likely follow suit.

Slavery, to cite another example, is once more a matter of ethics or social custom, the nature of the institution having varied greatly over space and time. Greeks who found themselves on the losing side of a war with Rome became slaves in Roman homes and tutors to the children of Roman nobles. As such, they commanded respect. Some were able to choose their own masters; there were limits to what an owner could demand; and terms of servitude were circumscribed.[169] But centuries later, as the Renaissance dawned and the condition of slaves began to deteriorate, church leaders modified their stance. Pope Pius II spoke against the institution in 1492, and half a century later, Paul III excommunicated all who took part in the slave trade. Further papal condemnation followed.[170] Did the church alter its teaching on a fundamental moral issue? Not at all, since it never, at any point, approved of conditions or practices that brutalized workers or abridged their God-given rights.

Simony and Indulgences

Luther had good reason to be concerned about ecclesiastical laxity and corruption. There were places where the sale of church offices (simony) was rampant, places too, where the preaching of indulgences was mishandled. One must distinguish, however, between a form of maladministration which has long since been rectified, and error in papal teaching, which never existed.

An indulgence may be defined as the remission of some or all of the temporal punishment due to sin following the performance of good works or the recitation of prayers. There is nothing wrong with such a concept. Peter and his successors were given the power to bind and loose, and much of the revenue from the granting of indulgences went toward the building of cathedrals, monasteries, schools, and universities. Furthermore, many who had been away from the sacraments were moved to return.

The most an indulgence ever promised was a lessening of one's term in purgatory commensurate with the mitigation of earthly penance. Since medieval penances could be severe, taking years to complete, "three hundred days" remission on a sentence of "six hundred days" meant something. And as for the "plenary" indulgence, which guaranteed remission of *all* punishment due to sin, it required total detachment from sin, something few penitents in any day or age could claim.

Unfortunately, the proceeds from the sale of indulgences were not always applied to the purposes for which they were earmarked.

---

[169] On slaves choosing their masters, see *This Rock* (July-August, 1996), p. 13 quoting St. Ambrose.

[170] Urban VIII in 1689, Benedict XIV in 1741, and Gregory XVI in 1838.

Secondly, it was not hard to gain the impression that an indulgence of say "three hundred days" meant so many days shaved from one's term in purgatory. Such, in turn, could be interpreted as a license to sin, though this was the farthest thing from the mind of the Church, which has always taught that time, as we know it, is nonexistent in the hereafter. Luther, in short, was not far wide of the mark on the first count. But he threw out the baby with the bath water when he denied two doctrines that are as defensible today as they were then: the authority of the Church to grant indulgences and the ability of men to profit spiritually from works.[171]

It should be noted in addition that the Church was not unwilling to admit administrative disarray. More than this, it sought to correct it at the Council of Trent (1545-63). In 1567, Pius V forbade any further collection of funds for indulgences. And more recently (1967), with an eye to the removal of coordinate grounds of misunderstanding, the rules were further altered to preclude reference to a specified number of days or years.[172] In sum, the church changed its tactics but not its teaching. Its basic position on sin and indulgences remains intact.

Annulments

Few developments have done more to undermine the church's claim to continuity of teaching than the escalating rate of annulments granted by American marriage tribunals in recent years. From a figure of 500 per annum in 1965, the number jumped to 48,000 in 1981.[173] A nation with only 5% of the world's Catholic population was suddenly granting 80% of its annulments. What happened to the church's traditional ban on remarriage after divorce? In the eyes of not a few, annulment is simply divorce, Catholic style.

The facts are as follows. A declaration of nullity (annulment) is nothing more than a statement to the effect that in the absence of certain preconditions, a marriage never took place. That is to say, the contract between consenting parties that is required for marriage was never valid. The Holy See, since time immemorial, has required

---

[171] Anne Carroll, *Christ the King: Lord of History*, 218.
[172] Karl Keating, *What Catholics Really Believe*, 93.
[173] In 1994, the number in the U.S. was 75,000 (75% of the figure worldwide).

certain things for a marriage contract to be valid. "Shotgun" unions, underage unions, and unions involving kinship of extremely close proximity do not qualify, nor do contracts in which either of the parties lacks full knowledge of matrimonial responsibility, full consent of the will, and a certain level of emotional maturity.

It goes without saying that in an age when fornication and cohabitation are rife, a great many men and women enter matrimony by the back door, so to speak. Full consent of the will is likely to be missing in certain cases just as there is bound to be a blurring of judgment when reason takes a back seat to passion. Parental negligence, faulty marriage preparation, and a materialistic ethos have all contributed to this sorry state of affairs.

The second thing to be borne in mind is that although Catholic teaching is divinely inspired, Catholic administration is not. The Church is a human institution with all that this implies. There can be little doubt that annulment tribunals in the world's most permissive nation have erred on the side of over-indulgence, and the Holy Father has expressed concern on more than one occasion about the resultant atmosphere of scandal, not to mention the tragic consequences affecting children and spouses. Accordingly, Rome has been seeking to eliminate unwarranted annulments by tightening the process whereby they are granted under canon law.

But annulments are *not* divorce, Catholic style. Catholic teaching has *not* changed. Nor can the Holy See be disqualified as a referee on faith and morals simply because its enforcement arm would appear to have been remiss.

One might add that there is nothing automatic about the process. According to recent estimates, only ten to twenty-five percent of Catholics who are civilly divorced have obtained an annulment, and for a person to be granted more than one is virtually unheard of.[174] Lastly, it should be said that, administrative problems aside, the church is stricter on matters relating to marriage and closer to the teaching of Christ and the Church Fathers than any other religious group.

---

[174] "Reasonable estimates on the percentage of divorced Catholics in America who have received a declaration of nullity range anywhere from 5% to 25%. I'll go with 10%." This is the opinion of canon lawyer and tribunal judge Edward Peters, as stated in "Annulments in America," *Homiletic and Pastoral Review* (November, 1996), p. 62.

Chapter 5

More on Catholicism and the Word

The Indissolubility of Marriage

Having made the case for continuity of papal teaching, we are free to resume our discussion of Catholicism and the Bible, taking into consideration a number of contemporary issues on which the Church has something to say, and there is no better place to begin than with the oldest and most venerable of all institutions, matrimony.

Most New Testament passages dealing with the subject are unequivocal when it comes to remarriage after divorce. Paul rules it out categorically. So does Jesus in the accounts given by Mark and Luke. Only in Matthew does one find a clause that calls for interpretation: "except in cases of immorality."[175] Over the years,

---

[175] See Mt. 5:32; 19:8-9; Mk. 10:10-12; Lk. 16:18; 1 Cor. 7:10-11; Romans 7:3. On the basis of one of the passages in Paul's first letter to the Corinthians (7:12-15), the Church reserves the right to dissolve a non-sacramental marriage between two unbaptized persons in accord with certain conditions: (a) there has been a sincere conversion to the Catholic faith by one of the parties, (b) the second party harasses the first in the practice of his or her faith to the point where it provokes grave sin, and (c) reconciliation appears impossible (see Canon Law, c. 1143-1150). One should note, however, that the Pauline Privilege has been a bit tenuous over the years. There is a certain hesitancy in Christian tradition about interpreting St. Paul's words to allow for more than separation, which is all that is explicitly granted. See *Jerome Biblical Commentary* (1968), 264.

Catholic commentators have taken such phraseology as a reference to the non-binding nature of premarital sex or incest, and translations are likely to read: "lewd conduct is a separate matter" or words to that effect. Protestant and Eastern Orthodox theologians, on the other hand, especially those ranged against the doctrine of indissolubility, view the phrase differently. Quite simply, they see it as an escape clause.

How well does the more indulgent of the two readings stand up under scrutiny? If nothing else, it leaves the word "immorality" open to an uncomfortably wide range of interpretation. Anything from a cutting tongue to chemical abuse could qualify. Protestants are also flying in the face of history. If divorce had been obtainable in the early church, surely one would find reference to it in the work of Mark, Luke, Paul, or one of the Fathers. Such, however, is not the case. Divorce is unheard of. Thirdly, Jesus made Genesis his criterion: "It was not so from the beginning" (Mt. 19:4); and Adam, as we know, had only one wife.

Approaching the question from another angle, one finds polygamy in the Old Testament. But no sage, judge, or prophet ever put away his wife to marry another. Furthermore, God is on record in the Book of Malachi as "hating" divorce (2:15-16).

From a purely secular standpoint, remarriage after divorce poses serious problems for children, as well as parents. Noel Coward and Clare Boothe Luce treat such quandaries charmingly in *Blithe Spirit* and *The Women*, and statistics bear out their message: the breakup rate for remarried divorcées is three or four times higher than it is for couples in their first marriage.[176] Henry VIII, perhaps the best known matrimonial rebounder of all time, wound up executing two of his wives. And who is not familiar with similar, albeit less dramatic cases?

According to a recent survey by researchers at the University of Virginia, 72 percent of all divorcées are convinced within two years of marital breakup that their divorce was a mistake.[177] All of which is corroborated by Diane Medved's study, *The Case Against*

---

[176] Cormac Burke, *Covenanted Happiness* (1990), 54.
[177] *National Catholic Register*, May 24, 1992, p. 5 – the percentage for men was also fairly high: 61%.

Divorce (1990), which reported that 75% of married divorcées do not recommend remarriage to others.

A third work by Judith Wallerstein, a University of California psychologist, found that only 10% of divorcées felt their life had improved; and many of these suspected they might be on the road to another crash.[178] Again there is corroboration. A *Newsweek* poll published in 1967 found divorced women a sorry lot. One in four turned to psychotherapy, and their suicide rate was three times above the average.[179]

Still other studies have shown that divorce is physically, as well as psychologically, devastating. Not only are the children of divorce more prone to drugs, suicide, crime, and poor grades at school; their parents are more likely to suffer early death from strokes, hypertension, respiratory ailments, and intestinal cancer.[180]

In sum, the Catholic position makes sense on practical, as well as moral and theological grounds.

Abortion

As in the case of remarriage after divorce, two other practices relating to human sexuality, abortion and artificial contraception, stand condemned on the twin grounds of scripture and human experience.

The Bible furnishes a wealth of quotation on the subject of when human life begins and hence what constitutes murder. Take, for instance, Psalm 71: "From my mother's womb you [God] are my strength." Isaiah, in chapter 49, has the Lord giving him his name and forming him as his servant in the womb of his mother. St. Paul refers to the Lord as one "who, from my mother's womb, set me apart and called me by his grace" (Gal. 1:15-16). The same sentiment appears in Jeremiah (1:4-5); and then there is Luke, who described John the Baptist as so "filled with the Holy Spirit from his mother's womb" that he "leapt" at the approach of the pregnant Mary (Lk. 1:15, 44). Add to this the fact that the Fathers of the

---

[178] See *Second Chances: Men, Women, and Children a Decade After Divorce.*
[179] Cormac Burke, *Covenanted Marriage*, 60.
[180] Philip Yancy, "God is Good for You," *Catholic Digest*, February 1992, p. 2.

Church are unanimous in their condemnation of abortion, and there is but one conclusion: the direct killing of a child — any child, at any stage of gestation, and for any reason — is an abomination. There will always be some who claim to know when human life, as compared with fetal life, begins. But this is casuistry. Common sense dictates that a baby who is human at six months is also human at six months minus a day. By the same token, one that is human at three months was human the day before. And so on all the way back to conception.

What we are witnessing today is a holocaust of unprecedented proportions, one which has taken the lives of tens of millions in the United States alone, and which continues unabated in spite of conscience, sacred scripture, and the unanimous verdict of the Fathers. Only in a culture of death could 95% of the abortions be for convenience (with 40% of them repeat performances by the same mother). Less than 5% involve rape, incest, or danger to the life of the mother.[181]

What many women do not know is that abortion can itself pose a threat to the life of the mother, and if not to her life, then to her general health. Don Feder, in *A Jewish Conservative Looks at Pagan America* (1993), cites a Canadian study of 84,000 teenage abortions that found laceration of the cervix in 12% of cases, hemorrhage (8%), infection (7%), and a perforated uterus (4%). Abortion has been known to cause clotting and strokes, and those involved are said to stand a 30% greater chance of developing breast cancer.[182] According to Dr. Bernard Nathanson, a leading OB-GYN, the number of serious complications from abortion every year in the United States runs into the thousands.

Emotional disturbances resulting from the killing of an unborn infant include guilt, depression, anger, lowered self-esteem, suicidal urges, emotional numbness, and sexual problems. Dr. Anne

---

[181] *The New York Times*, August 26, 1992, p. A23.
[182] Feder, *Conservative Jew*, 185-186. For the 30% figure on abortion, see a study by pro-life and pro-abortion scientists from Baruch College of New York and Penn State Medical School, which was published in the *Journal of Epidemiology and Community Health* (1996). *U.S. News*, November 7, 1994, p. 70, gives a figure of 50% on breast cancer.

Speckhard, Ph.D., in her study of Post-Abortion Syndrome, has listed, among the more common symptoms, hallucination (23%), perceived visitation from the aborted child (35%), nightmares (54%), feelings of craziness (69%), and preoccupation with the aborted child (81%). Speckhard found further that 61% of the cases increased their use of alcohol, 65% had thoughts of suicide, 69% were sexually inhibited thereafter, 77% experienced difficulty in communication, and 81% wept frequently.

Abortion rights, once hailed as a weapon in the campaign against illegitimacy, have failed to produce the expected benefits. Illegitimacy rates have actually risen, along with the rate of fornication, in the wake of easy access to abortion.[183]

Artificial Contraception

Much the same may be said of artificial birth control. The Old Testament contains at least three injunctions to "be fruitful and multiply." Two are addressed to Adam and one to Noah. But the importance that God attaches to human life and the sacredness of the procreative act is even more evident in God's striking down of Onan for a single act of birth control (Gen. 38:9-10). Onan may have been selfish in refusing to raise up issue to the wife of his deceased brother, as commanded by the Mosaic law. But the swiftness and severity of his punishment suggests retribution for the *way* in which he shirked his duty (i.e., by "wasting his seed").[184]

In the New Testament, Paul insists on the "natural use" of the woman by the man (Romans 1:26-27), and both he and John prohibit the use of "drugs," variously translated as "secret potions" or "witchcraft."[185] The Greek rendering of the word is "pharmakeia," and it generally referred to the mixing of potions for secret purposes. The fact that it is never mentioned except in connection with sexual license and that such potions are known to have been mixed in the first century to forestall pregnancy, as well as to terminate it, is strongly suggestive.

---

[183] *Wall Street Journal*, August 9, 1994, p. A13.
[184] Charles D. Provan, *The Bible and Birth Control* (1989).
[185] Galatians 5:20 and Revelation 9:21.

Contraception was also referred to in Christ's day as having resort to "magic" or "sorcery," and again, one can point to evidence of Christian prohibition.[186] A real thorn in Peter's side on his visit to Samaria was one Simon Magus, a "sorcerer" or "magician" (RSV) by Luke's account and the only person denounced to his face as hell-bound by the first pope (Acts 8:20). The closest one comes to Simon Magus is Bar-Jesus, also called Elymas, a name meaning "sorcerer" (or "magician") who practiced his arts on Cyprus, an island known for harlot priestesses and the worship of Venus. And what becomes of Elymas? He is struck blind by Paul for trying to thwart evangelization (Acts 13). Most likely, Christianity affected his pocketbook. Scripture must also be read in conjunction with texts such as the *Didache*, which instructs first-century readers as follows: "You shall not use magic. You shall not use drugs. You shall not procure abortion. You shall not destroy a new-born child."[187]

Jesus himself, in restoring marriage to its original state — as it was "from the beginning" — described husband and wife as "one flesh" (Mt. 19:5), a phrase that can hardly be applied to couples using prophylactics.

Among the Fathers of the Church, all who refer to such practices as abortion, sterilization, and artificial contraception condemn them out of hand, and the list is long. It includes Clement of Alexandria, Lactantius, Chrysostom, Jerome ("Some go so far as to take potions that they may ensure barrenness and thus murder human beings almost before their conception"), and Augustine ("Cruel lust resorts to such extravagant methods as to use poisonous drugs to secure barrenness or else, if unsuccessful in this, to destroy the conceived seed").[188]

---

[186] Revelation 21:8 and 22:15. See also John F. Kippley, *Marriage is for Keeps* (1994), 78; John A. Hardon, *The Catholic Catechism* (1975), 367.

[187] *Didache*, II, 2 (quoted in Hardon, *Catholic Catechism*, 367). It should be added that sorcery, which is linked with sexual wantonness and adultery in the Old Testament, carried the death penalty (Isaiah 57:3; Malachi 3:5; Ex. 22:17).

[188] Clement of Alexandria (in *The Instructor of Children*, 91 A.D.), Lactantius (in *Divine Institutes*, 307 A.D.), Chrysostom (in *Homilies on Matthew* and *Homilies on Romans*, 391 A.D.), Jerome (*Against Jovinian* and Letter 2, sec. 13, dated 393 and 396 respectively), Augustine (*Against Faustus*, 400 A.D.; *Marriage and Concupiscence*, bk. 1, ch. 17 [15]; and *The Good Marriage*, 401 A.D.), and Caesarius (*Sermons*, 522 A.D.). For these and other citations, see *This Rock*, January, 1996, pp. 40-42. See also Provan, *The Bible and Birth Control*.

The argument is sometimes made that moral precepts, as found in scripture, must change with changing times. But this renders virtually all of the gospel null and void. Even if Jesus had never stated that "Scripture cannot be broken" (John 10:35) and that "not one jot or tittle from the law will pass away" (Mt. 5:18), even if Paul had not added that "Jesus Christ is the same yesterday, today, and forever" (Hebrews 13:8), assuring us that "all scripture is inspired by God and useful for teaching" (2 Tim. 3:16), and even if Jesus had not appealed to the way things were at the beginning of time (Mt. 19:4), we know that human nature remains constant. Furthermore, there is legitimate reason to doubt that times have in fact changed when it comes to the fear of procreation. Ancient fears may have been different from ours, but they were real.

The received wisdom is that while children may have been regarded as an asset before the Industrial Revolution, such was not so on its aftermath. But where is the evidence? Anti-natalism is mentioned by the Greek Polybius (150 A.D.), by Pliny the Younger (c. 100 A.D.), and by Luther ("today you find many people who do not want to have children"). Pliny tells us that his was an age "when even one child" was "thought a burden preventing the rewards of childlessness," and according to the eminent Puritan, Richard Stock (d. 1626), "many men and women, though they desire some children, [do] not [desire] many." All of which makes perfect sense considering that the rate of infant mortality was far higher and child bearing attended by far greater risks then than now. If children were so widely welcomed and regarded as such a blessing in days of old, why is it that Church Father after Church Father felt it necessary to inveigh against contraception?[189]

Church teaching has always allowed couples to practice abstinence during the woman's fertile cycle if the circumstances are sufficiently serious, if abstinence is mutually agreeable, and if it is not an occasion of sin.[190] At the same time, it has been constant in affirming that every child is a gift from God, as well as a gift *to* God. The Lord loves every one of us, and if all of us, whatever our

---

[189] Provan, *The Bible and Birth Control*, 50-52, 58.
[190] See Frederick W. Marks, *A Catholic Handbook for Engaged and Newly Married Couples* (1997), 75-78.

background or condition, are equal in his sight, if all of us are born with equal access to heaven, there can be but one conclusion.

Frequently, one hears it said or implied, "My wife and I couldn't begin to cope with another child" or "my wife would go insane with another pregnancy ... already we lack adequate space, privacy, and comfort." From a strictly human point of view, who can argue? But where does Christ come into the picture? Did he not caution his followers against murmuring, "What shall we eat? Or what shall we drink? Or what are we to put on? ... Your heavenly father knows that you need all these things," he assured them. "Seek first the kingdom of God and his justice, and all these things shall be given you besides" (Mt. 6:31-34). Why did Our Lord commend a poor widow for giving away all that she had to live on if he did not want us to rely implicitly on his all-embracing mercy and generosity (Mk. 12:44)?

There is an old Spanish proverb to the effect that "Every child comes with a loaf of bread under its arm." As believers in divine providence, we can be sure that God will not send any family more than it can bear, and bear profitably. Parents of large families are remarkably consistent in attesting to the fact that they didn't know how they could possibly manage with a third or fourth child ... until the child in question came along; then, somehow, they managed, and managed well. What today's world needs above all else is a countercultural faith in the efficacy of God's grace, along with a willingness to harken to a voice in the realm of faith and morals that is insulated from politics and public opinion.

Even on the human plane, it is no secret that contraception is hazardous to a woman's health. Barrier methods subject her to a higher risk of preeclampsia, one of the leading causes of morbidity. She also faces intrauterine growth retardation and prenatal mortality. Hormone contraception not only causes blood vessel tumors in the lower coronaries, high blood pressure, and clotting (strokes). It can also lead to skin pigmentation, gum bleeding, jaundice, baldness, sterility, depression, herpes, loss of libido, visual defects, and problems with breast feeding. Intrauterine devices, for their part, tend to cause excessive bleeding, perforation of the uterus, and pelvic inflammatory disease.[191] Women have died from

---

[191] H. P. Dunn, M.D., *The Doctor and Christian Marriage* (1992), 62-70.

use of the pill, and they are still dying. It is associated with heart disease and an increase in certain kinds of cancer; and fifty percent abandon it due to a string of unpleasant side effects including irritability, depression, weight gain, and loss of libido.

As in the case of abortion, there are likely to be emotional problems as well. Contraception can be a bone of contention and hence a cause for divorce. Consider the following scenarios: (1) One partner wants to contracept; the other doesn't; and they argue; (2) He wants to contracept and she agrees but fails to follow through properly. He demands an abortion; (3) He wants a child; she has reservations; and nothing comes of their intercourse. He becomes suspicious because she is not opposed to contraception in principle and may be using it surreptitiously; (4) After five years of contraception and saving for their child's Ivy League education, a couple finds they cannot conceive. They are desolated. Fifteen percent of couples find themselves in this situation automatically, and contraception can itself be a cause of sterility; (5) After five years of contraception or use of the pill for "spacing" purposes, a couple finds that they can have only boys (or girls). What must they think? (6) After five years of contraception, a child is born, but it is their last, and they desperately want another. Again, one can only imagine what they must think. (7) After five years of contraception, a child is born, but it is deformed in body or spirit, and again, it is their last.

Without a doubt, children can be a source of discord, as well as a burden, especially if they are not properly managed. But studies show that they are more likely to be the glue that holds a shaky marriage together. Those with large families who welcome children early are less likely to go their separate ways. Many a husband or wife who decided to stay the course "for the sake of the children" proves grateful in the long run that he or she did not make any rash decisions.

It is always risky to tamper with the procreative process. Four centuries ago, a French queen by the name of Catherine d'Medici tried to force God's hand. Desperate for heirs to the throne, she put herself under the care of "magicians," and eventually she bore children. But all of them, without exception, came to tragic and premature ends.[192]

---

[192] Carroll, *Christ the King*, 246.

With the spread of contraception, sexual intercourse is regarded by many as simply another form of recreation, and with results that are predictable. Among the practices to which separation of the unitive and procreative functions of the marital act leads are masturbation, sodomy, sterilization, and adultery, not to mention pre-marital sex, abortion, and illegitimacy (how can teenagers be denied the pleasure their parents enjoy if physical satisfaction is the be-all and end-all?).[193]

When Planned Parenthood commissioned a series of studies by Johns Hopkins University in 1971 and 1976 under the auspices of the National Institute of Child Health and Human Development, the findings appeared in a publication of the Alan Guttmacher Institute called *Family Planning Perspectives*, and they were revealing: during the period 1971-76, the number of teenagers in family planning programs quadrupled (from 300,000 to 1,200,000). During the same interval, premarital intercourse was up 41%, premarital pregnancy increased 45%, and the number of illegitimate births rose by 18%. In 1971, 39% of teenage out-of-wedlock pregnancies ended in abortion. In 1976, the figure was 51%.[194] Although one cannot "prove" cause and effect, the facts all point in one direction.

Pope Paul VI, who condemned contraception in his 1968 encyclical, *Humanae Vitae*, was remarkably prescient. His forecast: artificial contraception would lead to a rise in conjugal infidelity and a general decline in morality. He also foresaw a rapid rise in abortion, the growth of a movement to legalize euthanasia, resort to forcible sterilization by totalitarian governments, and a surge in violence against women.[195] Human bodies, he warned, would be

---

[193] *Wall Street Journal*, August 13, 1993, p. A6. The only method of birth control approved by the Catholic Church is Natural Family Planning: and it is not for most couples under most circumstances, only when there are "grave" reasons (*Humanae Vitae*, No. 10). By pinpointing a woman's fertile period with a high degree of accuracy, it allows those willing to engage in periodic abstinence to do so effectively. And because it is completely natural, there are no adverse side effects. Far from lessening libido, it tends to have the opposite effect. See Marks, *A Catholic Handbook for Engaged and Newly Married Couples*, 75-78.

[194] Dr. Eugene F. Diamond, "Teaching Sex to Children," *Columbia Magazine*, June 1981.

[195] *Wall Street Journal*, August 13, 1993, p. A6.

treated as machines — to wit, *in vitro* procedures and surrogate motherhood. Every one of his predictions has come true.[196]

Trial marriage, another product of the pill-driven revolution, was supposed to afford singles a better chance of finding the right mate. In fact, the divorce rate is 50 to 70% *higher* for those who cohabit than it is for couples who live chastely before marriage.[197] Sin is never a good place to discover the truth! During the period 1965 to 1975, which registered a dramatic increase in use of the pill, divorce rates shot up, doubling and then leveling off in 1975 just when everyone who might conceivably wish to use it was doing so. Again, although a cause and effect relationship cannot be "proven" it is strongly indicated by the evidence.

Interestingly enough, every one of the Protestant reformers without exception condemned artificial birth control, with John Wesley going so far as to warn that those who practiced it would lose their soul. Similarly, all major religious bodies condemned it until Anglican leaders broke ranks in 1930 and decided to sanction it for "serious reasons." In effect, this was a blanket endorsement, for whose reasons are not serious? And since then, the Anglican communion has suffered the sharpest drop-off in membership since its inception under Henry VIII.

To recapitulate, the Catholic position is firmly grounded in scripture and tradition. It recognizes God as a loving, provident father; and it shields men and women alike, along with their offspring, from physical and psychological harm. Beyond this, it honors the age-old principle that the end does not justify the means — one may not commit an evil act in order to do good. To steal, even with the intent of putting a worthy student through college, is wrong.

The Cost of Discipleship

There is no question that God's will in matters of procreation involves sacrifice, even heroic sacrifice at times. But this should

---

[196] I am indebted for much of the above information to Dr. Janet E. Smith of the University of Dallas, in particular her tape, "Contraception: Why Not?"

[197] *The New York Times*, June 9, 1989, p. A1; *Our Sunday Visitor*, December 27, 1992, p. 23; *National Catholic Register*, May 7, 1989, p. 5.

come as no surprise. Jesus himself could not have been more direct: "He who wishes to be my disciple must take up his cross and follow me." Which recalls another of Our Lord's sayings: "They will persecute you as they persecuted me."[198] Satan is the "prince of this world," he insisted, and those who resisted evil would be dragged before courts and "hated by all."[199] Tradition has it that no fewer than ten out of twelve apostles, following in the footsteps of Stephen and John the Baptist, gave their lives.

Here again, the Catholic Church, more than any other, conforms to the Christian blueprint, as well as to the spirit of apostolic times. Among Peter's successors, an estimated twenty-four were martyred; six more were murdered; thirteen were tortured; five were exiled; and nine were imprisoned and physically abused. Few pontiffs over the years have escaped being the butt of ridicule and vilification.

But it is not only on the level of the papacy that one finds heroic witness. Scions of noble families in Elizabethan England gave up wealth, social standing, even life itself, to cling to the faith of their fathers. Fifteen bishops resigned when Elizabeth came to the throne, and of these, twelve were imprisoned (one for twenty-four years) because of their refusal to recognize a worldly ruler as head of the Church.

British North America during the seventeenth and eighteenth centuries down to the era of the American Revolution presents a similar picture. Catholics could not attend Mass in most colonies without risking arrest, and nowhere could they vote or hold public office. In Maryland, the children of Catholic widows could be taken into custody by the state, just as there were places where Catholics could not own a gun or horse.

Because the American Revolution owed its success in such large measure to French and Spanish aid, things changed somewhat after 1776. But the bias continued. In Boston and Philadelphia during the decade 1834-44, a Catholic convent school, along with Catholic churches and a Catholic seminary, were burned to

---

[198] John 15:20.
[199] John 14:30; 15:19; 16:11; 1 John 5:19.

the ground. Catholics could not vote or hold office in New Jersey until mid-century, and in New Hampshire, they could not serve as governor or stand for election to state office until 1876.[200]

Turning to the Orient, twenty-six believers were crucified at Nagasaki in 1597, and in the years that followed, Japanese Catholics were hunted like wild animals by the hundreds of thousands. Korea alone has produced 103 martyrs since 1840, while in contemporary China, an estimated six to eight million underground Catholics persevere in the practice of their faith at considerable risk.

One of the more curious features of Church history is the fact that Catholics have been relegated to pariah status even in places where they comprise a sizable portion of the population. During the French Revolution, an estimated 40,000 died for their faith, including dozens of priests and nuns. Catholic schools, monasteries, nursing homes, and hospitals were closed, and hundreds of churches and cathedrals were desecrated. Anticlericalism of a similar kind swept Mexico during the 1920s, Cuba forty years later, and Germany under Bismarck and Hitler. Or take Republican Spain, where 7,000 priests and nuns were slaughtered in 1936.[201]

Eastern Europe under Soviet occupation from the end of World War II until the 1980s presents yet another chapter in an ongoing story of pain and sacrifice. People seen going to church in countries such as Hungary and the German Democratic Republic were almost certain to be denied high-level employment, along with access to the universities. In Lithuania, hundreds of thousands of faithful Catholics were executed or deported to Siberia.

The vitriol of anti-Catholic exposés is again without parallel. During the nineteenth century, a woman by the name of Maria Monk masqueraded as a disillusioned ex-nun and made a living retailing fictitious horror stories about convent life. Today, Tony Alamo and the California-based Chick Publications carry on the tradition of Catholic defamation.

One exposé in particular stands out: Loraine Boettner's *Roman Catholicism*, published in 1962. Scholarly, but at the same

---

[200] Francis X. Curran, S. J., *Catholics in Colonial Law* (1963).
[201] See Warren Carroll, *The Last Crusade* (1996).

time popular, it has sold over a hundred thousand copies, and it is riddled with distortion. Boettner cites the opinion of various church Fathers on the apocryphal books (p. 82) while omitting the testimony of these same authorities on the Eucharist and papal infallibility. Catholic reverence for the pope is described as "adoration" and the Catholic ideal for women as "merely to bear and to drudge" (pp. 129, 165). This may reflect Boettner's view of homemaking and the raising of children, but it has little to do with Catholicism. The church has always had the highest regard for consecrated virginity, and it looks upon homemaking and the rearing of youngsters as among the most skilled and important tasks in the world.

There are other chestnuts: "Romanists, having been to Mass … can do about as they please the remainder of the day" (p. 184) and "no masses are said without money" (p. 185). Penance is said to be a substitute for repentance (p. 191) and communion hosts are described as wafers "dropped" into one's mouth (p. 194). One error follows upon another. Boettner treats Fatima, Lourdes, and Guadalupe without acknowledging Catholic claims or dealing with the facts. At the same time, one is led to believe that it is a mortal sin for a Catholic to "enter a Protestant church" (p. 296) and that Catholic Uniate churches differ in doctrine, as well as liturgy, from Western-rite churches (p. 309).

Why such calumny? Is it because an organization which claims to be "the way, the truth, and the life" displays enviable unity in an age of fragmentation? Or perhaps because it calls for discipline in matters of procreation and family life? In 1995, when the U.N. Conference on Population met in Cairo, delegates from the Holy See found themselves practically alone in opposing an agenda of radical birth control, including forced abortion and sterilization. Amidst a raucous chorus of denunciation and with only a smattering of support from a handful of countries, mostly Moslem, the Holy Father did what he could.

Here, as elsewhere, those who stand for less are less persecuted. Not that Christians of other denominations have not suffered and given their lives. They have, and their record is far from ignoble. In the main, however, it is Catholics who have borne the brunt of persecution around the world and Catholics who continue to bear it.

Rich and Poor

Often the case is put that Protestant nations are better off materially and, on the whole, more literate than their Catholic counterparts. Northern Europe is undeniably more prosperous than southern (Catholic) Europe. Britain's standard of living exceeds that of Ireland. Similarly, Spain and Portugal, the most Catholic countries of Europe for decades, were also its least affluent.

At the time of the Eastern Orthodox split with Rome (1054), dissident areas positively shone in riches and literati. Constantinople, the first major city to turn its back on the Holy Father, was wealthier than Rome, just as schismatic Alexandria and Antioch were culturally superior to Milan and Lyons. Whether one compares North America with South America or northern Germany with southern Germany, the lesson seems everywhere the same: prosperity and Protestantism go hand-in-hand.[202]

The argument is appealing. But the more one studies it, the more one finds that it proves the exact opposite of what is intended.

Jesus had a special regard for the poor and, by extension, poorer nations, calling them "blessed" and identifying with them by opting personally for a life of poverty.[203] It was the "little" people, rather than the "wise and prudent," whom he called his own, and he dubbed Satan "the prince of this world" (John 16:11). Nothing, if not consistent, in this regard, he not only warned against the fear of poverty but urged his apostles to give away all that they possessed, saying that it was "harder for a rich man to enter the kingdom of heaven than for a camel to pass through the eye of a needle" (Mt. 19:24).

How can one view the wealthier classes or nations as "better off" when Jesus underscored the seductive power of money (Mt. 13:22)? Graphic pictures are drawn in the gospels of affluent individuals consigned to hell: for instance, the parable of the rich man and Lazarus (Lk. 16) and the portrait of the prosperous farmer who builds extra barns for his bountiful harvest so that he can "eat, drink, and be merry" (Lk. 12).

---

[202] See, for example, pp. 4, 144, 215-16, 273, 445, 449.
[203] Luke 6:20; 12:33 and James 2: 1-7.

Did Paul, who dubbed love of money "the root of all evil" (1 Tim. 6:10), not paint God's prophets as "destitute, distressed, and afflicted" (Hebrews 11:37)? When Jesus came to Jerusalem, he stayed at the home of a leper in the humble suburb of Bethany (Mk. 14:3), and Peter, visiting Joppa, accepted the hospitality of a lowly tanner (Acts 9:43).

The question is: which nations would Jesus regard as "blessed" today? If Paul were to return to the missionary trail, where would he feel most at home? Athens enjoyed a reputation for literacy and sophistication; yet according to Luke, it was "wholly given to idolatry" (Acts 17:16), and Paul described it as sterile by comparison with lower-class Corinth. In like vein, the church of Macedonia, among the poorest and least educated, proved to be the most generous (2 Cor. 8:2), while Jerusalem, greatest of Jewish metropolises, was condemned by our Lord as the place that "killeth the prophets and stonest them that are sent to thee" (Mt. 23:37).

Consider, in addition, the fate of the Sadducees, all of them members of the social and financial elite. Not one, so far as we know, was sufficiently detached from worldly pursuits to be open to Jesus' message. Priests like Zachary converted (Acts 6:7). Pharisees like Saul and Nicodemus weighed in on the side of Christ (Acts 15:5). Even publicans. But never, to our knowledge, a Sadducee. They rejected the bulk of the Bible, accepting only its first five books, just as they disdained belief in angels and an afterlife. In short, they were theologically liberal, and Jesus told them that they were "entirely mistaken" (Mk. 12:27).

Wealth and salvation need not be mutually exclusive. Abraham acquired a reputation for holiness, and he was well off. So was Job. Nicodemus, who felt constrained to come to Jesus at night, and Joseph of Arimathea, a member of the Sanhedrin who claimed Jesus's body and laid it in a tomb, may likewise have found favor on the day of judgment. Judas, on the other hand, was infatuated with money. At the very least, he turned into a thief who, far from fleeing occasions of sin, remained in his post as treasurer, managing Jesus' finances and dispersing funds to the needy (John 12:6). If any apostle was worth knowing from a worldly point of view, it was Judas. Yet his name is synonymous with treachery.

It may require a stretch of the imagination to go from Judas to the rich nations of the world. But the fact is that those bent upon a high "standard of living" in pre-Christian times gravitated to Sodom, Babylon, and other lush marts which no longer exist. The Old Testament describes merchandising as dangerous to the soul, and what better proof than the current plight of the American family, languishing, as it is, in a modern-day Mecca of materialism?[204] As Lord Acton observed, "Power corrupts ... absolute power corrupts absolutely." Professor Paul Vitz has written in a somewhat more specific vein:

> We all know that it is hard for a rich man to get to heaven. I'm certain that it is even harder for a Ph.D. The problem for the Ph.D. — and I really mean to include doctors and lawyers and professionals of all types — is the problem of pride and will.[205]

Returning to the gospel, Jesus adds a twist to his message when he says, "That which is exalted in the sight of men is an abomination before God" (Lk. 16:15). For Paul, God uses the poor of the world "to shame the rich" (1 Cor. 1:27-31), and James has God choosing "the poor of this world to be rich in faith" even as the rich "weep and wail" over their "impending miseries" (James 2:5; 5:1).

Why, it may be asked, should one go out of one's way to aid the poor if they are so fortunate? The reason is simple: it is God's plan. Although the Lord is perfectly capable of looking after his own, he has chosen to make us instruments of divine providence because he knows that we need the poor as much as the poor need us. We may not think of ourselves as the principal beneficiaries of our own charity. But clearly we are. Similarly in the case of evangelization. If the good pagan is as eligible for a berth in heaven as the exemplary Christian, why trouble to convert him? First, because Jesus, before ascending to heaven, commanded us to do so: "Preach to all nations." Secondly, because the pagan will be happier after conversion — truth invigorates the soul by setting it free

---

[204] Sirach 26:20.
[205] Paul Vitz, *Psychology as Religion* (1977), 29.

(John 8:32). But not least of all because faith, like joy, increases the more it is shared. We are really evangelizing ourselves when we reach out to others.

Pacifism

The Church's position on pacifism, of a piece with its stand on poverty and evangelization, takes its cue from scripture. Quakers, Jehovah's Witnesses, the Amish, and a number of other sects see the Fifth Commandment, in conjunction with Jesus' "Turn the other cheek," as ruling out military service. They also recall Christ's surrender to Jewish authorities without lifting a finger and his warning when Peter cut off the ear of Malchus, servant of the chief priest: "Those who live by the sword will die by the sword."[206]

There are several things worth noting in this connection. Canaan was won by force with the blessing of the Lord, indeed the Old Testament is replete with allusions to the legitimacy of soldiering, among them Ecclesiastes 3:8: "There is a time for war and a time for peace."[207] Can anyone forget Elijah's slaughter of hundreds of false prophets at the Lord's behest? Pacifism on the part of Jesus would have been such a radical departure from Jewish tradition that one would expect clear delineation of it in the work of Matthew, Mark, Luke, and John. Yet what do we find? The New Testament portrays soldiers as model citizens. At the foot of the cross, it is a military man who exclaims, "Truly, this man was the Son of God!" (Mk. 15:39). Jesus commended a Roman centurion for having more faith than anyone in Israel (Lk. 7:9). And Jesus' cousin, John the Baptist, when asked by soldiers for advice, told them to be content with their pay (Lk. 3:14).

A Roman centurion, Cornelius, was the first Gentile to be converted to Christianity, and Peter, who converted him, did not counsel him to resign his commission. Jesus' attitude was "render to Caesar the things that are Caesar's" (Mt. 22:21), and the theme is

---

[206] Matthew 26:52 and Revelation 13:10.
[207] See also Joshua 6:17; 8:1-2, 22-24; 10:30, 32-33, 40. Elijah slew all 450 prophets of Baal, along with many prophets of the Asherah, after discrediting them on Mount Carmel.

further developed by Paul: "Not without reason does it [the civil authority] carry the sword; for it is God's minister, an avenger to execute wrath on him who does evil" (Romans 13:4). Paul specifically urges his flock to "be subject to princes and authorities, obeying all commands" (Titus 3:1).

Why, if Jesus was a pacifist, did two of his apostles bring swords to the Last Supper (Lk. 22:38)? And why did he say that after he was delivered into the hands of men, "Let him who has no sword sell his tunic and buy one" (Lk. 22:36). To be sure, when Peter struck Malchus, he was reproved for taking the law into his own hands. But Jesus also said, "Bear with them thus far" — in effect, "Hold your fire; I am committed to the carrying out of my Father's will."[208]

Would a doctrinaire pacifist condone violence, even implicitly, and season his discourse with martial imagery: "If a strong man fully armed guards his courtyard, his property remains undisturbed" (Lk. 11:21). There is the parable of two armies (Lk. 14:31-32), the tale of an unmerciful servant "handed over to the torturers" (Mt. 18:34), and Jesus' description of a tough master who has his lazy servant slain.[209]

Faith and Works

A good deal of what passes for criticism of Catholic theology, whether pacifist or otherwise, relies on caricature. Among other things, the Church has been accused of giving the impression that if one attends enough Masses, says enough prayers, lights enough vigil candles, and drops enough bills into the collection basket on Sunday, this will open the gates of heaven.

Such teaching has never been part of the deposit of faith. On the contrary, Catholicism has always held that without Christ's sacrifice on Calvary, no one could enter heaven, and further, that good works are vain without the right disposition. What it has not

---

[208] Luke 22: 49-51.

[209] Luke 19:27. See also Matthew 22:7 and 13. For Paul's use of martial imagery, see Ephesians 6:10-17; Romans 13:12; I Thessalonians 5:8; 2 Timothy 2:4; 4:6. For John, see Revelation 9:16.

done is to teach that works are of no avail — "faith alone saves" — and that once one accepts Christ as one's personal savior, salvation is assured — "once saved, always saved."

"Faith alone" Protestants cite Paul's dictum that "whoever calls upon the name of the Lord shall be saved" in concert with other passages.[210] But like the pacifist, they are selective, overlooking Jesus' "Not everyone who says to me, 'Lord, Lord,' shall enter the kingdom ... but [only] he who does the will of my Father" (Mt. 7:21) and "He who loves me keeps my commandments" (repeated five times in the fourteenth chapter of John). The gospels are replete with statements to this effect.[211]

James is unequivocal: "Faith without works is dead."[212] Accordingly, he stresses the need to resist temptation: "Blessed is the man who endures temptation; for when he has been tried, he will receive the crown of life."[213] John, too, emphasizes works.[214] Finally, one can appeal to Peter: God "judges according to each one's work."[215]

---

[210] Romans 10:13. For other such quotes, see Romans 3:26; 7:20-23; 8:30; 9:14-18, 30, 32; 11:6.

[211] For example, that we will be judged according to our "conduct" on the day of reckoning (Matthew 7:21; 16:27; 25:34-36; Luke 6:46-49). For additional examples, see Matthew 7:21 ("not everyone who says 'Lord, Lord' shall enter the kingdom of heaven, but he who does the will of my father in heaven" with the verses that follow); Luke 6:46-49 ("Why do you call me 'Lord, Lord' and do not practice the things that I say? ... He who has heard my words and has not acted upon them is like a man who built his house upon the ground without a foundation"); John 14:21, 23 ("He who has my commandments and keeps them, he it is who loves me.... If anyone loves me he will keep my word"); John 15:2 and 10: ("Every branch in me that bears no fruit he will take away.... If you keep my commandments you will abide in my love"); John 15:14 ("You are my friends if you do the things I command you"); Matthew 12:46-50 ("Who is my mother and my brethren? ... Whoever does the will of my father in heaven, he is my brother and my sister and mother"); and John 5:29 ("They who have done good shall come further unto resurrection ... but they who have done evil unto judgment").

[212] James 2:14, 19-20.

[213] James 1:12-13.

[214] I John 1:6-8; 2:4 and 6; 3:7; 5:2-3; 3 John 11; Revelation 20:13; 22:12-13.

[215] 1 Peter 1:17. For Paul, see 2 Cor. 11:15; Romans 2:6-8, 10, 13; 6:23; 11:22; Hebrews 10:26-31.

"Once saved, always saved" Protestants believe that adult conversion guarantees salvation provided it is sincere. But if this is so, why did Paul worry about being rejected by God?[216] If anyone underwent conversion, it was he. Yet in one of his letters, he compares life to a race in which the finish line is not crossed until the final moment.[217] "Be not deceived," he exclaims, "neither fornicators nor idolaters nor adulterers ... shall inherit the kingdom of God."[218]

Confusion arises because Paul, in his eagerness to attract Gentiles, held that circumcision and other Mosaic practices relating to diet and purification were not needed for salvation, a stand approved by Peter after his vision in Joppa. This is what he means when he writes that "faith alone" is required. The subject is a difficult one; meanings can be opaque; and hence Peter's warning, adduced earlier, that Paul can be confusing to those who are ignorant or unstable in their faith.[219]

There was a time when Calvinist divines regarded all mankind as predestined from birth to heaven or hell. For scriptural underpinning, they relied on texts such as Romans (1-11) and Ephesians (1:4): "He predestined us" and "chose us in him before the foundation of the world." This is simply another instance of failure to scan scripture in its entirety, for there is ample evidence, often in Paul's own words and certainly in the words of Jesus, that no one is predestined in the sense commonly understood.[220]

Catholic teaching on faith and works is happily situated between extremes. While admitting man's unworthiness and dullness in the absence of divine grace, it has not repudiated the early Christian notion, heavily undergirded by scripture, that such grace is on tap for all who call upon the name of the Lord. Much less does it shrink from the principle that one must endeavor to cooperate with it. God did not tell us to *strive* for honesty or to *try* not to

---

[216] 1 Cor. 9:27; Philippians 3:12.

[217] 1 Cor. 9:24-27.

[218] 1 Cor. 6:9-11.

[219] 2 Peter 3:16.

[220] See Romans 11:22; Colossians 1:23; 1 Timothy 2:4; Luke 7:30; 22:22. See also 2 Peter 3:9.

kill, or to *do our best* not to commit adultery. Rather, it was "Thou shalt not." Much is expected from him to whom much is entrusted, and each of us is born with the gift of free will.

Fidelity to Scripture

Non-Catholic scholarship, while strong in some areas, has not been without its lapses. Luther doctored the Bible to suit his theology when he altered the phrase, "by faith" to read "by faith alone," and such practice has not been uncommon among dissenters. Protestant versions of the Bible featured an appendage to the Lord's Prayer which recent scholarship has shown to be unwarranted: "For thine is the kingdom and the power and the glory."[221] Catholic editors, by contrast, have remained faithful to the text even when inconvenient, as in the case of "brothers and sisters" (referring to Jesus' cousins).

While Protestants have stripped the Old Testament canon of some of its most delightful and instructive books, labeling them "apocryphal," Rome has been properly circumspect, recalling that when New Testament writers cited Hebrew scripture, their source was generally the Septuagint, the Greek translation of the Hebrew Bible; and the Septuagint, like Catholic editions, contained the deuterocanonical (apocryphal) books.[222]

The consonance of Catholicism with the substance and tone of God's word is evident in other ways as well. All seven of the Church's sacraments are Bible-based; and in keeping with Paul's counsel to "drink a little wine" (1 Tim. 5:23), along with Jesus' changing of water into wine, Rome has never proscribed alcoholic

---

[221] See Curtis Vaughan, ed., *The New Testament from 26 Translations* (1967), 22; Currie, *Born Fundamentalist*, 164; Rumble and Carty, *Radio Replies*, I, 121. As another case in point, the King James version of the Bible changed Paul's "Whoever shall eat *or* drink unworthily" to "eat *and* drink" (Rumble and Carty, *Radio Replies*, I, 182 – italics added).

[222] Currie, *Born Fundamentalist*, 104-107. Three hundred out of three hundred and fifty Old Testament quotations, as found in the New Testament, are taken from the Septuagint (Rumble and Carty, *Radio Replies*, II, 118).

beverages.[223] Neither has it discouraged popular belief in the healing power of relics, recalling that a corpse, on making contact with Elisha's bones, resurrected; a woman, after touching the hem of Jesus' garment, was healed; and articles of Paul's clothing wrought miraculous cures when applied to the sick.[224]

Miracles

We have come a long way with our blueprint analysis. But we mustn't stop here. No examination of the harmony between Catholicism and scripture would be complete without recalling Jesus' pledge to his followers that they would work miracles (Mt. 10:1; Mk. 16:17). They fully expected their ministry to be accompanied by cures, signs, and wonders (Acts 4:30); and in point of fact, it was. How many of today's religious denominations identify with Christ's promise? How many can point to a steady stream of phenomena indicative of divine intervention across a stretch of two thousand years, much of it heavily documented? To be sure, the individual Catholic is not bound to believe in any miracle beyond those found in scripture. But the Church as a whole has so believed; it continues to believe; and such belief is eminently biblical.

Since this is not a book about miracles, we shall pass over reports of the stigmata (wounds of crucifixion in the hands and feet); likewise cases of saints' bodies remaining incorrupt long after burial despite normal contact with the elements. Instead, we shall concentrate on an extraordinary series of events which took place at Guadalupe, Lourdes, and Fatima.

Guadalupe

The story of Guadalupe began on December 9, 1531, when an Indian by the name of Juan Diego reported seeing the Blessed

---

[223] Scriptural basis for the sacrament of Extreme Unction or Anointing of the Sick: James 5:14-16; also Mark 6:13. For Baptism: Mt. 28: 19-20 and John 3:5. For Confirmation: Acts 8:14-17 and other passages similar to it. On being a "soldier of Christ," see Ephesians 6:13-17.

[224] 2 Kings 13:20-21; Luke 8:43-45; Acts 19:12.

Mother on the outskirts of Mexico City. After requesting that a church be erected in her honor for the greater glory of her son, she gave a sign of her presence. Juan was instructed to gather flowers out of season on a rocky hill where they were not ordinarily found. Discovering a variety of blossoms, he cut them and wrapped them in his cactus cloak or "tilma," which he then unfurled before the eyes of an astonished bishop. Witnesses were doubly amazed to find emblazoned on his garment a miraculous image of the Virgin, magnificent in detail, perfectly proportioned, and inexplicable to the present day in terms of chemical composition.

For the next 116 years, Juan's cloak was fully exposed. Anyone who cared to see it, kiss it, or touch it in any other way could do so. Science is at a total loss to explain how cactus fiber could have withstood such exposure for much more than twenty-five years, especially as it was unprotected from air, moisture, fluctuations in temperature, and smoke from candles. In 1921, a bomb exploded directly beneath the tilma without doing it the slightest harm. Although a metal crucifix only a few feet away was bent practically in half, the glass enclosure surrounding the popular object of devotion remained perfectly intact. Juan's cloak is still on display for all to see, as well preserved and captivating as ever.

Lourdes

Lourdes, a village situated in southern France at the foothills of the Pyrenees, is another site worth visiting for the aura of holiness that pervades it. During evening candlelight processions, when rosaries are recited in many languages, the effect is incredibly moving.

In 1858, a devout peasant girl by the name of Bernadette Soubirous reported seeing Mary and hearing a plea for repentance, prayer, and mortification. Mary promised a great miracle on a certain date, and when the day arrived, a large crowd gathered and gazed in awe-struck wonder as Bernadette, instructed by the Blessed Mother to dig in the ground with her bare hands, did so, and a spring of water suddenly gushed forth.

Ever since, at fairly regular, albeit lengthy, intervals, pilgrims to Lourdes have reported spectacular cures after bathing in the water.

Not a single infection has ever been transferred from one patient to another, even though the water into which invalids are lowered with suppurating sores and contagious germs is changed only twice a day. As for the cures themselves, they defy all the laws of medical science. Lourdes' Institute for research allows unlimited access to the records of all persons said to have been cured; its scientific character has yet to be impeached; and no cure certified by Church authorities has ever been discredited.

According to the gospel of John, "an angel of the Lord used to come down at certain times" and work cures at the Pool of Bethesda in Jerusalem (5:4). Perhaps this same angel is still coming down!

Fatima

As in the case of Lourdes, it is a young girl who captures the attention of the world from the Portuguese village of Fatima in the year 1917; and again, the story is uncomplicated. Lucia dos Santos and two other children announce that the Blessed Virgin has appeared to them requesting prayer and penance and presenting them with a vision of suffering souls in hell. They also report Mary's promise of a great sign or miracle to occur on October 13. So great is the curiosity of the populace that on the appointed day, an estimated 70,000 persons are on hand, including atheists, agnostics, and anti-clerical journalists. A terrific downpour soaks spectators to the bone. But it is followed by a truly marvelous sight: the sun breaks through, dances, spins around, and throws off brilliant rays of light in every color of the rainbow. It then gives the appearance of hurtling toward the earth at such enormous speed that many fall to the ground in terror.

Such is the bare outline of facts as attested by those present at the "Miracle of the Sun," including eyewitnesses within a radius of twenty kilometers. Even the editor of Lisbon's largest daily who, before the 13th had been an outspoken critic of the church and the children, published a moving first-person account in *O Seculo*.

Three other aspects of the miracle of Fatima are worth recalling. Lucia quoted the Virgin as having promised that two of the young seers would soon be called home to heaven in answer to their request and that Russia would become a seedbed of Satanic deception leading many astray. According to Lucia, Mary also fore-told a second world war close on the heels of the first unless people turned back to God. Remarkably, it was not long before two of the children died of natural causes. Almost immediately, Russia went communist, following Lenin's takeover. And within a generation of the First World War came the Second.

Since 1917, Marian apparitions have been reported with in-creased frequency in places as far removed as Garabandal, Spain and Akita, Japan. Again, it must be said that Catholics are under no obligation to credit such reports. But the Church would not be in full harmony with the spirit of the Gospel if it did not take cog-nizance of them and if such signs did not occur periodically under its spiritual aegis, since they were the promise of the Savior and the hope of the Twelve.

Mary the Model

The common denominator of Guadalupe, Lourdes, and Fatima is, of course, Mary. Jesus could have appeared in person or sent an angel. Why did he dispatch the woman greeted by Gabriel two thousand years ago as "full of grace"? All we know for certain is that, in the long history of the world, only two women were born without stain of sin, Eve and Mary, and both had free will. One said "no" to God, the other "yes," and in both cases the conse-quences were incalculable.

Some believe that Catholics, in according Mary such a promi-nent place in their devotional practice, detract from the glory due to Christ alone. Why, they wonder, should she be called "Mother of God" when she was only human? What basis is there for as-suming that she was born without stain of original sin (the dogma of the Immaculate Conception)? Or for insisting on a virginal con-ception of Christ? What, in addition, is the basis for Catholic be-lief that Mary was taken directly to heaven at the end of her life (the doctrine of the Assumption) and that she remained a virgin after the Nativity when there is mention in the gospels of Jesus' "brothers and sisters"?

Why such intense concentration on Mary generally when so little is known about her and she receives scant attention in Holy

Scripture? Why recite "Hail Marys" more often than the Lord's Prayer, as in the rosary? And why are statues of Mary so often displayed in Catholic churches?

In answer to the first query, Catholics regard Mary as "the Mother of God" only in the temporal sense formulated by the Council of Ephesus (431), and this because her son *was* and *is* God, one of three persons in the Blessed Trinity.

In response to allegations of undue emphasis, it should be clear to any careful inquirer that Catholics do not worship Mary; they merely venerate her, and never in such fashion as to slight her divine son. There may be statues of Mary in Catholic churches, but the crucifix is there as well, centrally located for the most part, along with the tabernacle containing Christ's body and blood. There are also extensive readings from both the Old and New Testament every Sunday so that regular Mass attendees are exposed to everything in scripture that they need to know. Finally, the "Hail Mary," which is based on the gospel of Luke (1:28, 42), is not an integral part of the Mass, whereas the "Our Father" is. Even in the rosary, eleven out of fifteen decades commemorate events in the life of Christ.

This is as it should be, and, one might add, as Mary herself would have it, since she, like any other mother, wishes to have the attention of friends and associates focused on her son. Marian apparitions have brought millions of nonbelievers into the Church founded by Jesus.

Devotion to Mary has waned in recent years, and this is unfortunate, as there is no greater exemplar of the Christian life, no better antidote to misguided feminism, than the woman who brought Jesus into the world and raised him to manhood. Self-pity finds little room beside the multiple crosses borne by this faithful, self-effacing Lily of Juda. Consider, to begin with, her conception of the Christ child, seemingly illegitimate in the eyes of the world, followed by three taxing journeys during pregnancy, and a stable, instead of an inn, at the time of delivery. In swift succession came exile to Egypt with an infant at the breast and the shocking news of Herod's slaughter of the Innocents. How many mothers of these poor unfortunates had she come to know during her sojourn in Bethlehem? And was she not aware that such carnage would never have occurred had it not been for the Nativity? Simeon's dire prediction that a sword would pierce her heart, coupled with Herod's execution of a beloved relative, John the Baptist, must have added materially to her woes.

Five times she staggered under a sense of maternal loss: once when Jesus dropped out of sight for three days; again when he left home to become an itinerant preacher; a third time when the townsfolk of Nazareth sought to kill him; yet again when he expired on the cross; and finally when he ascended to heaven. It is hard to imagine any feeling other than desolation on such occasions. Yet nary a tear by any of the accounts that have come down to us. What faith! What fortitude! What resignation to the will of God!

Was there any pain felt by her son that did not cut her to the quick? How she must have trembled at reports of assassination plots. How she must have suffered during the mock trial on Holy Thursday, then again at the news of its verdict and the prospect of crucifixion. This was the sword Simeon had predicted, this the loss by a widowed mother of an only child at the height of his powers.

Nor was this yet the end. Like hammer blows came the stoning of Stephen, the execution of James, the expulsion of Christians from Palestine, and a second forced exile, this time to Ephesus with John. Assuming she lived through the Roman persecution, there was no way of saving the lives of Peter and Paul; neither could she shield her adopted son, John. Although an attempt on his life failed — his captors reportedly lowered him into a cauldron of boiling oil — he had to live out the remainder of his days on the island of Patmos, and Mary's life on earth ended, as it began, in total obscurity.

"He whom the Lord loves he chastizes," we read in the Epistle to the Hebrews (12:6). And what better example, when we find ourselves under siege, than Mary, who represents human nature unalloyed and who traversed the proverbial vale of tears in union with her son. If anyone demonstrated the price of discipleship and showed her children the way, it was she.

Our Blessed Mother

She predicted, in a moment of divine inspiration, that "all generations" would call her "blessed" (Lk. 1:48), and so it came to pass. We can do no less, as "blessed" was the title given her by

Gabriel, as well as by Elizabeth (twice) and an unidentified follower of her son.[225]

St. John adds to the brilliance of his gospel likeness when he describes her as a queen "clothed in the sun" with the moon at her feet and on her head a crown of twelve stars (Rev. 12:1). Not even Abraham, Moses, or Elijah, in all their glory, were ever so pictured. At the same time, John casts her as nemesis to Satan and the mother of all who stand against the power of evil (Rev. 12:17). Need one add that when Jesus "gave" her to John during the crucifixion (John 19:27), he was giving her to all mankind?

Small wonder that so many of the world's heroes called upon her in their hour of need. Columbus not only visited her shrine in Zaragoza before weighing anchor for the New World, but his flagship, the *Santa Maria*, was named after her, and his crewmen prayed the rosary. During the Battle of Lepanto (1571), which broke the naval power of Islam, the rosary was again prayed, and with great fervor, while the banner borne by the Christian flagship was that of Our Lady of Guadalupe.

The Virgin Birth

The virgin birth is implicit in Mary's response to Gabriel (Lk. 1:26-38) when taken in conjunction with Joseph's reaction and the phrase, "He knew her not until she brought forth her first-born son" (Mt. 1:18-25). Isaiah predicted that "a virgin" would conceive and bear a child whose name would be Emmanuel, meaning "God with us" (7:13-14); and while "alma," the noun used by Isaiah, was a loose term signifying young woman (married or unmarried), "virgin" is clearly the meaning of the word in this case because the Septuagint opts for the unambiguous Greek rendering of "virgin."[226]

Interestingly enough, Muslims are as adamant as Catholics on this score, holding that Mohammed's favorite daughter, Fatima, conceived two of her sons virginally. An entire chapter of the Koran is devoted to Mary, and it is not uncommon for Muslims touring Rome to visit churches dedicated to Our Lady.

---

[225] Luke 11:27 (for the unidentified follower).
[226] On wide Jewish readership, see entry in Valentine's *Jewish Encylcopedia*.

The Immaculate Conception

When Mary's freedom from the stain of original sin was proclaimed a dogma by Pope Pius IX on December 8, 1854, reactions within Catholic circles varied, while critics outside the fold took it as simply another instance of papal manufacture of doctrine.

Ultimately, the question must be decided in light of one's confidence in papal teaching authority. This is not to suggest, however, that scriptural support is by any means lacking. Since Mary is identified as the bride of the Holy Spirit — it is he who "overshadows" and impregnates her (Lk. 1:35) — it is perfectly logical to view her as the beneficiary of special graces and immunities from the moment of conception. Gabriel's greeting, "Hail, full of grace," is significant inasmuch as the normal thing for an angel to say would be "Hail, Mary." What does it mean to be "full of grace"? What other person in scripture is so-called?

Earlier in history, when God tells the serpent, "I will put enmity between you and the woman, between your seed and her seed" (Gen. 3:15), the word "enmity" implies special enmity. And who is "the woman" if not Mary, especially when one juxtaposes Genesis with John's account of the marriage feast at Cana, in particular Jesus' query to his mother, "What wouldst thou have me do, woman? My hour has not yet come" (2:3)? Mary, "the woman," calls forth the first of her son's miracles and launches him on a career that will "crush" the head of the serpent (Gen. 3:15).

Twenty-four years before the Holy Father decided to elevate traditional belief in the Immaculate Conception to the level of a doctrine, a Parisian woman by the name of Catherine Labouré witnessed an apparition of Our Lady crushing the head of a serpent and referring to herself as "conceived without sin." Catherine had a medal struck with these very words on it, and so many miracles were worked on behalf of those wearing it that it came to be known as "the Miraculous Medal." Equally telling are the events of Lourdes which occurred four years after Pius' proclamation and in which Mary identified herself to Bernadette as "the Immaculate Conception."

Admittedly, Pius' decision cannot be justified on the basis of apparitions or miracles any more than it can be upheld solely on the basis of scripture. In dealing with twilight areas, one must have recourse to a higher authority, and this is where Christ's decision to entrust the keys of the kingdom to a single man, Peter, comes in, along with his promise of the Paraclete (John 14:16-17; 16:12-13).

The Assumption

The dogma that Mary was assumed directly into heaven at the end of her life rests almost entirely on tradition, coupled with the interpretive power of the papacy. Yet if Enoch and Elijah could go directly to heaven, then Mary, the mother of Our Lord, would surely qualify.[227] There is no resting place or tomb containing her remains, and nothing could be more consistent with her preservation from the stain of original sin than belief in her exemption from physical decay since bodily corruption was a legacy of Adam and Eve (Gen. 3:19).

Jesus' "Brethren"

Another Catholic tenet that draws on tradition, albeit to a lesser extent than that of the Assumption, is the belief that Mary remained a virgin. When Helvidius took exception to this notion toward the end of the fourth century, he was excoriated by Saint Jerome, who labelled his dissent "novel," "wicked," and "a daring affront to the faith of the whole world." Jerome was able to quote Ignatius, Polycarp, Irenaeus, and Justin Martyr, while Helvidius had to rely on Tertullian, a heretic by the time he died, along with Victorinius, whose opinion Jerome was able to show had been misconstrued.[228] It was not much of a contest.

The position upheld by Jerome is found in all of the earliest creeds. Mentioned at the Council of Constantinople in 397 A.D., it was proclaimed a dogma of the Church at the Fifth Council of Constantinople (533 A.D.). After 649, when the Lateran Council condemned dissenters, the consensus that emerged was so firmly

---

[227] For reference to Enoch, see the eleventh chapter of Hebrews. See also Genesis 5:24.

[228] Karl Keating, *Catholicism and Fundamentalism*, 286-87.

grounded that neither Luther nor Calvin nor Zwingli thought to question it a thousand years later.[229]

Certain passages do seem to suggest that Jesus had brothers (e.g., Mark 6:3). But one must bear in mind that Aramaic, the language spoken by Jesus and the first generation of evangelists, had no word for cousin. Consequently, "brother" was used as a catchall to denote cousin, close associate, coreligionist, neighbor, stepbrother, or kinsman.[230]

Peter called Paul his "brother" (2 Peter 3:15), just as Paul referred to his fellow Christians as "brothers" (Romans 15:14). After the Resurrection, Jesus instructed Mary Magdalene to tell his "brothers" [brethren] that he was ascending to his Father.[231] At one point, when Jesus was teaching, someone interrupted him to say that his mother and brethren had come to have a word with him. Whereupon he asked, "'Who is my mother and who are my brethren?' And stretching forth his hand toward his disciples, he said, 'Behold my mother and my brethren! For whoever does the will of my Father in heaven, he is my brother and sister and mother'" (Mt. 12:47-50).

Equally suggestive is the fact that while Matthew refers in one passage to James and Joseph as Jesus' "brothers" (13:55), he identifies them elsewhere as sons of another Mary.[232] We know, too, from the gospel of John that there were several Marys.[233]

Granted, Mark, Luke, and John wrote in Greek; and Greek, unlike Hebrew and Aramaic, had separate and distinct words for brother and cousin. Nevertheless, the Septuagint uses the Greek word for brother even in cases where Hebrew scripture clearly means "cousin," and one can argue that New Testament writers

---

[229] *Our Sunday Visitor*, January 8, 1989.

[230] See, for example, Romans 9:3; Matthew 5:22-24.

[231] John 20:17. See also Acts 1:15-16. There are plenty of examples in the Old Testament of generalized use of the word "brother." Compare, for instance, Genesis 11:26-28 with 14:14 (on Lot's relation to Abraham) and see Genesis 29:15 wherein Jacob is called brother to his uncle Laban. See also 2 Esdras 5:7; Jeremiah 34:9; 2 Samuel 1:26; 1 Kings 9:13; 20:32; 2 Kings 10:13-14; and Amos 1:9 as cited in Keating, *Catholicism and Fundamentalism*, 282.

[232] Matthew 27:56. See also Mark 15:40.

[233] See John 19:25; also Matthew 28:1.

were simply following the example of the Bible they knew best.[234]

Why, if Mary had not taken a vow of virginity, did she respond to Gabriel's promise with such incredulity: "How can this be?"[235] As a maiden about to be married, she had every right to anticipate motherhood. Why, too, if she bore other children — at least six by the Protestant reading of Mark 6:3 — did Jesus entrust her to John at the foot of the cross? Would a devoted mother forsake children and grandchildren to take up residence with the male associate of one of her sons, as Mary did when she made her home with John (John 19:27)?

Dissenters latch onto another elliptical phrase, "He [Joseph] knew her not *until* she brought forth her *first-born* son" (Mt. 1:25 — italics added). The operative point here is that the word "until," in early times, didn't necessarily signify subsequent action. In the second book of Samuel, for example, the childless Michal, daughter of Saul, is said to have "had no children until the day of her death" (6:23). Or take the 34th chapter of Deuteronomy, verse 6: "No man knows the site of Moses' grave until this present day" — his gravesite has *never* been known. As for the expression "first-born," it was a title routinely given to the child that opened the womb. In no way did it imply the birth of others.[236]

Mary and Christian Unity

Lastly, it should be mentioned that Marian devotion constitutes a crucial link between western and eastern Christianity. Orthodox churches are resplendent with icons of Mary, and it would be hard to conceive of fruitful ecumenical dialogue between East and West without a shared devotion to the Blessed Lady.

---

[234] See Keating, *Catholicism and Fundamentalism*, 283.
[235] Luke 1:34. See Keating, *Catholicism and Fundamentalism*, 283.
[236] See Exodus 13:2; 34:20; Numbers 3:12; Joshua 17:1.

Conclusion

God promised Abraham that his descendants would be a blessing to all nations and as numerous as "the sands on the seashore," and both of these promises, remarkably, have been fulfilled.[237] Catholicism, with over a billion adherents, exceeds the membership of all Protestant and Orthodox churches combined. Its houses of worship are everywhere, its Masses offered in virtually every tongue. Loss of the Eastern Orthodox in 1054 was more than offset by the reconquest of Spain. Similarly, German, Swiss, Scandinavian, and English defection during the sixteenth century was compensated by the conversion of millions in the New World.

Not that truth is a matter of counting heads. Majoritarian views are seldom lofty, and there are times when they must be resolutely resisted by the officers of God's army. Underlying much of the weakness of modern-day Protestantism is precisely its vulnerability to public opinion. The cross that surmounted Christian churches in pre-Reformation times has been replaced oftentimes by the weathervane, symbol of prevailing sentiment. Well-meaning ministers and their families are beholden to lay governing boards whose decisions may hinge on the whim of a slender majority. At the same time, the trend toward autonomy of individual congregations poses a mounting threat to unity.

Significantly, among all churches, only one has stood rocklike against the moral meltdown of modern times. And while many who call themselves Catholic have turned a deaf ear to Rome, there is at least such a thing as "Catholic teaching." In the present age of science, technology, and widespread skepticism, an organization

---

[237] Genesis 22:17-18.

claiming to be "the way, the truth, and the life" continues to face down obdurate rulers and to cling to such doctrines as papal infallibility and transubstantiation. Over the years, its leadership has approved places of pilgrimage, endorsed reports of divine apparitions, validated records of miraculous cures, and canonized thousands of saints without taint of graft, deception, or malfeasance. Cynics have spared neither time nor money in search of hoaxes, and they have found none.

Imagine our Lord on an international tour of inspection. What would he think of the oldest and largest church purporting to teach in his name? If nothing else, he would be impressed by the dramatic increase in religious vocations in Africa, South America, Central America, and Southeast Asia.[238] If he were to join the annual pilgrimage from Notre Dame Cathedral in Paris to Chartres — seventy miles on foot in three days — he would be gratified to discover that the number of pilgrims has risen in recent years from a mere handful to many thousands. Shuttling to Korea, he would be pleased to find a fellowship that is at once robust and growing; and in the Philippines, he would be welcomed by a group that is highly energized and powerful, if threatened.

Making the rounds in Western Europe and North America, he would be dismayed by the ravages of a secular incubus that has infected all mainline faiths. Yet even here he might not be altogether disheartened, recalling that some of history's greatest institutions took root at times and places when morality was at low ebb. France, during the tenth century, was such a place, a spiritual wasteland, when the Duke of Aquitaine founded his celebrated monastery at Cluny (910 A.D.). And from that time on, reform swept the land like wildfire. Fifteen hundred branches sprouted from the motherhouse, and three of Cluny's monks were elected pope. Judging from the many religious orders that have put down

---

[238] Under the pontificate of John Paul II, they are said to have risen by a factor of 60-65% – see *Homiletic and Pastoral Review*, May 1996, p. 62. From 1970 to 1994, when vocations in the United States and Western Europe were precipitously in decline, vocations in the Church as a whole were rising: up 394% in Africa, 253% in South America, 165% in Central America, and 152% in Southeast Asia (see *Our Sunday Visitor*, November 10, 1996, p. 13).

roots in affluent countries in recent years, not to mention a host of publications, media networks, educational institutions, and apologetics groups — all newly enlisted in the cause of orthodoxy — the Cluny phenomenon appears to be once again in train.

The Jewish Connection

Our Resurrected Lord would note with satisfaction that Catholic houses of worship have retained a sense of divine indwelling in keeping with God's command: "Let them make me a sanctuary that I may dwell among them" (Ex. 25:8). Holy water would be familiar to him (Num. 5:17; 8:7). Likewise, genuflection, which would call to mind standard devotional practice in the Holy of Holies. Jesus himself knelt when he prayed in the Garden of Gethsemane (Lk. 22:41), and his followers fell down before him to do him reverence.[239]

Lest it be forgotten that Our Lord, as a devout Jew, followed Old Testament liturgical practice, it should be recalled that he not only instructed fellow Israelites to go to the high priest and offer for their purification "the things Moses commanded" (Mk. 1:44). He also made it clear that his disciples were to do "all things" prescribed by the Pharisees, while disregarding their example (Mt. 23:3), for he had come not "to destroy the Law or the Prophets," but rather to "fulfill" them, and "not one jot or one tittle" of the Law would be abolished until all things had been accomplished (Mt. 5:18).

Not surprisingly, when Marcion, a second-century reformer, whom we had occasion to mention earlier, tried to dissociate Christianity from its Jewish past, specifically its commitment to the Hebrew Bible, he was thoroughly repudiated.[240]

Jesus would appreciate the refinement of Catholic vestments, altar ornamentation, and attention to architectural design, as Jewish priests were enjoined to wear the finest cloth and to adorn God's

---

[239] On genuflection and kneeling, see Nehemiah (or 2 Esdras) 8:6; Revelation 4:9-11; Mark 1:40; 10:17; John 9:35-38.

[240] The Gnostics in general rejected the Old Testament. See Newman's *Essay on the Development of Christian Doctrine*, p. 92.

dwelling with acacia wood, gold, silver, and precious stones.[241] Among the Twelve, Judas alone balked at expenses connected with divine worship, suggesting that the money might be better spent on the poor (John 12:5).

The fragrance of incense rising heavenward at Benediction and the washing of the celebrant's hands at Mass would be reminiscent of frankincense burning in the temple precincts and the ritual purification of the high priest, while the vigil lamp, attesting to the presence of consecrated bread, would remind him of the sanctuary light of the temple, which burned twenty-four hours a day over the Ark of the Covenant alongside the "bread of the presence" and cups of wine (Lev. 24). If he were exposed to bell ringing at the most solemn moment of the Divine Liturgy, it would recall to him the tinkling tunic worn by the high priest which allowed worshipers to "hear" his movement in the Holy of Holies. One is aware, too, that Jesus fasted and attended weekly assembly, as required by the Mosaic law, just as he made annual pilgrimages to the holy places. As a devout Jew, he would also have prayed for the souls of the faithful departed.[242]

Absolutely central, however, to any comparison between Catholicism and Judaism is the concept of sacrifice. At the time of Christ, Jews had what was called the Zebah Todah, or sacrificial thank offerings, at which those who brought victims to the temple consumed part of their offering. Animals were delivered daily to be immolated in expiation for sin — sheep, turtledoves, rams, and oxen. Parts of these victims then became the portion of the priestly classes. A lamb was sacrificed on the altar every afternoon of the year, and during Yom Kippur, the sins of the people were laid onto the back of a goat (the scapegoat) which was then banished to the wilderness or pushed over a cliff.

There is little corresponding to any of the above customs in the current practice of most Jews and Protestants. But every day,

---

[241] See also Sirach, ch. 45; Ex. 35:9.

[242] Luke 1:9; Ex. 35:28 (on incense and the vigil lamp); Sirach 45:9 (on bells); Ex. 40:32 (on hand washing); and Lev. 8:9 (on the wearing of a miter); Lev. 23:3; Lk. 4:16; and Heb. 10:25 (on the obligation to attend Sabbath Assembly); Lk. 2:41 (on pilgrimages).

in the Holy Sacrifice of the Mass, Christ himself is offered by the priest in an unbloody representation of his death on Calvary in atonement for the sins of mankind.

Jesus, observing the way the priest raises his hands over the bread and wine prior to consecration, would recall what Moses did during Joshua's battle with the Amalekites. He raised up his arms in blessing, and every time they sagged in fatigue, Joshua lost ground. Consequently, Aaron and Hur bolstered the outstretched forearms of their leader until victory was assured (Ex. 17:8-13).

Our Lord would also be taken by the Catholic "kiss of peace" — a handshake in the West and a bow in the Orient — since this was the way hosts greeted their guests in his day, and he was known to resent its omission (Lk. 7: 44-46).

Lastly, we have it from Paul that Jesus would endorse the Church's stand on mixed marriage (2 Cor. 6:14-18) in the same way that he would identify with Catholic claims to the fullness of truth. The Jews regarded themselves as a chosen people directly in touch with Almighty God through the Pentateuch, the prophets, and the Ark of the Covenant; and their high priest had the power to condemn dissenters to death.

Saint Watching

Since ours is an age when personal virtue and attention to spiritual detail are apt to be dismissed as the stuff of mere fiction, Jesus would appreciate the Church's insistence on holding up to young and old alike role models of sterling character.[243] He would also recognize the current roster of saints as perfectly in keeping with ancient catalogues of heroes as found in the Book of Sirach and the Epistle to the Hebrews.

What better way to internalize that most difficult of Jesus' teachings, love of one's enemy, than by recalling the way Joan of Arc echoed the words of Stephen, the first Christian martyr: "Lord, forgive them, for they know not what they do." It was thus that Thomas More marched to the scaffold. Without a trace of bitterness, he told his executioners that he hoped to meet them "hereaf-

---

[243] Hebrews, ch. 11 and Sirach, chapters 44-50.

ter in heaven."[244] Similarly in the case of Edmund Campion under Elizabeth I, sixteen Carmelite nuns from Compiègne, who went to the guillotine during the French Revolution, and Emperor Maximilian of Mexico, who died magnanimously at the hands of anti-clerical forces. Pope Pius VII (1800-1823), after being kidnapped and humiliated by the armies of Napoleon, used his papal office to plead for mercy when Napoleon was himself taken captive, and later he offered to shelter the Bonaparte family. John Paul II, for his part, granted pardon to a would-be assassin after the latter had lodged a bullet in his chest.

While all but one of the individuals cited above was a priest or nun, that one, Thomas More, has been canonized. Clearly, saints do not have to be priests or members of religious orders. Representative figures of the laity have been beatified and canonized by the hundreds. St. Luchesio was a merchant, Dominic Savio, a schoolboy, St. Margaret of Cortona, a reformed prostitute. St. Nicholas of Fluë, widely regarded as the father of Switzerland, was, like so many others, a layman. Nor should one forget St. Macrina, mother and grandmother of five other saints, including Basil the Great, founder of eastern monasticism.

Many among the ranks of the canonized were nobly bred; but again, not all. Don Bosco, founder of the Salesian Order, and Pope Pius X (1903-14) happen to have been sons of peasants. Anastasius is known to us as a fuller. Zita was a serving girl, Gratian a fisherman. The company of saints includes a porter, Conrad of Parzliam, and a locksmith, Baldomenus. St. Vincent de Paul was the only member of a family of six whom his father could afford to send away to school.

It was widely assumed that the Church must have erred when figures like St. Philomena and St. Christopher were "dropped" from the official calendar of saints. But this is not so. The process known as canonization did not originate until 993 A.D., and it was not reserved to the papacy until 1171. George, Christopher, Philomena, and others like them, are simply names about whom little is known and for whom there is no documentary record, only a tradition that grew into popular devotion during the early centu-

---

[244] Bernard Bassett, *Born for Friendship*, 198 (on More).

ries.[245] The Church denies neither their existence nor their worthiness. It merely acknowledges belatedly that there is insufficient evidence to verify the legend.

Presence

Another feature of modern-day Catholicism certain to make a favorable impression on Jesus is its presence. The Lord made himself available to his followers at all times, even when inconvenient. And so it is with his Church. Because its tabernacle contains the Blessed Sacrament before which worshippers kneel in adoration at all hours of the day and night, Catholic places of worship are more frequented, and hence more accessible, than those of any other faith. Priests are never off duty; confessions are heard weekly; and the Divine Liturgy is offered every day of the year, often in several languages — forty-two in the diocese of Los Angeles alone.[246]

The Man from Nazareth went everywhere and mingled with everyone, ministering to young and old, rich and poor, the healthy and the sick. He was as anxious to heal the mentally ill as he was to engage intellectuals, and his apostles were a mixed bag socially. As St. Paul described the fledgling community in Corinth, there were "not many wise according to the flesh, not many mighty, not many noble" (1 Cor. 1:26); and this is the way it remains in the Catholic fold. One may enter any large urban church on a Sunday and find a quintessentially Christian amalgam; bagmen and millionaires, high-school dropouts and Ph.D.s, men and women of diverse ethnic backgrounds, along with spokesmen for every ideology. Not long ago, I chanced to pass an abortuary in New York City and was struck by the presence of a priest, a nun, a child, and several laymen, all praying the rosary. No one else. Church officials were the first to operate a state-certified clinic for the treatment of AIDS patients, and of course Catholic chaplains are found on every battlefield, in every hospital and prison, and at the scene of every fire.[247]

---

[245] John J. Delaney, *Dictionary of Saints*, 13.

[246] *National Catholic Register*, April 26-May 2, 1998, p. 14.

[247] In New York City, St. Elizabeth's Church has Masses for the deaf, and St. Clare's Hospital opened the first state-certified clinic for AIDS treatment.

One for the Books

Catholicism continues to set records. Pope John Paul II, laborer, linguist, writer, actor, sportsman, and philosopher, has drawn by far the largest crowds in history — four million, by one count, in Manila alone. And Mother Teresa of Calcutta will be remembered as the most prodigious social worker of her time. Where else does one find the ten to twelve years of training that go into the making of Jesuits and Legionaries of Christ?

Scanning the pages of history, where, outside the Church, does one encounter the burning zeal and heroism of the Jesuit martyrs of North and South America? Who can come even with a Francis Xavier or Matteo Ricci? Within ninety years of Xavier's arrival in Japan, there were approximately 1,000,000 Japanese Christians and 250 churches. Where is the counterpart to Peter Claver, nobleman turned Jesuit who braved the stench of slaveholds aboard newly arrived galleons in 17th century Cartagena to ameliorate the lot of African chattel?

Father Damien, celebrated missionary and minister to outcasts, risked his life and eventually lost it assisting lepers on the island of Molokai. So unique was the settlement he founded that Robert Louis Stevenson, after spending twelve days on Molokai, was moved to write:

> I have seen sights that cannot be told and heard stories that cannot be repeated. Yet I never admired my poor race so much nor (strange as it may seem) loved life more than in the [Catholic] settlement.

Damien, he declared, was "a man with all the grime and paltriness of mankind, but a saint and hero all the more for that."[248]

Elizabeth of Hungary, after being widowed at the age of twenty-two, declined a marriage proposal from Frederick II, emperor of all Christendom, because she yearned for a life of humble service to the poor in imitation of Christ. St. Margaret of Hungary, a con-

---

[248] Stevenson's *Letters*, edited by Colvin, III, 151-53, 214.

temporary, did the same thing for similar reasons, turning down an offer of marriage from the King of Bohemia.

Thomas More stands at the very top of the list of persons who sacrificed for the faith. No one gave up as much as More. But there were others. Court favorite George Calvert (Lord Baltimore) resigned his post as secretary to the king to become a Catholic, while another convert, Philip Howard, Earl of Arundel (1557-95), spent the last eleven years of his life in the Tower of London, stripped of his estates and title as Duke of Norfolk and barred from all contact with family owing to the uncompromising staunchness of his faith. Nor are Calvert and Howard the only prominent Protestants in a Protestant milieu known to have embraced Catholicism with little to gain and everything to lose. John Dryden passed up the chance to remain poet laureate and royal historiographer of England.[249] Edmund Campion, John Henry Newman, and John Knox left behind friends, relatives, and illustrious careers. Ben Jonson, next to Shakespeare the leading dramatist of Elizabethan England, risked his livelihood to enter the Church, and from there he went on to write his best plays, *The Alchemist* and *Volpone*.

Evidence has surfaced that Shakespeare was himself a Catholic. Considering the age in which he lived, his work is consistently sympathetic to Rome. Both his pastor and schoolmaster were ardent Catholics who resigned their posts in Stratford rather than apostatize, and the bard himself wrote a scene for a play, *Thomas More*, which was later banned. Some accounts suggest that he served as baptismal sponsor for one of Jonson's children, Mary.[250] Be it as it may, Jan Vermeer, a convert prominent in the world of painting, braved the suspicion and hostility of Protestant Holland to attend Mass, while Sigrid Undset of Norway converted several years before winning the Nobel Prize for Literature.

Along a similar but slightly different line, it is worth noting how often Catholic artists have clung to their faith in a sea of militant Protestantism. William Byrd, foremost musical composer un-

---

[249] Dryden was dismissed in 1688 by William of Orange as poet-laureate and royal historiographer owing to his Catholicism.

[250] Smith, *The Other Side of Christ*, chapter 8 ("Shakespeare's View of the Narrow Path").

der Elizabeth I, risked professional ruin by hewing to the ancient faith, while Alexander Pope, best-known of all poet-satirists of his time, gave up a formal education in England, along with residence in London, with the same end in view.[251]

The list is long and the phenomenon inexplicable except in terms of the attractive power of truth. The only reason we do not have more Calverts, Howards, and Newmans is that authentic Christianity clashes with the way of the world. As Pascal remarked, "There are two types of men: those who are afraid to lose God and those who are afraid they might find him." The minority who harkened to the voice of the living Christ were not, like the leaders of the Pharisees and Sadducees, wedded to social status and the indulgence of human frailty. Rather, they were seekers bent upon finding the most direct route to God, firm in the belief that nothing is more liberating in the long run than the unvarnished truth. In exchange for it, they were willing to sacrifice everything; and so it is with true seekers in every age.

None of this is to deny that the Church is made up of human beings prone to error when it comes to matters of discipline and organization. No group or individual has a monopoly on merit, and there can be no doubt that individual priests, groups of bishops, and even popes, have fallen from grace. Admittedly, too, there is an esprit de corps and dignity about the way many of our non-Catholic brethren conduct themselves that can only be winning. Orthodox Jews exhibit a reverence for the Sabbath and a respect for learning — loving God with one's whole mind — that is sadly lacking in many Christian quarters today. Protestants, for their part, have placed a wholesome emphasis on Bible study and adherence to the work ethic.

But having said this, Catholicism occupies high ground. It is still the rock of rocks and, as such, the most powerful voice in the world for the sanctity of human life, the integrity of the family, and the existence of objective truth. By comparison with the clarion

---

[251] Pope's witticisms include, "To err is human, to forgive divine" and "fools rush in where angels fear to tread." He was the first English poet to enjoy contemporary fame on the Continent and to have his poems translated into modern, as well as ancient languages.

tone and unswerving directness of papal pronouncement on key moral issues, the witness of other denominations is likely to appear timid, lukewarm, and inconsistent. A century and a half ago, the eminent historian and man of letters, Lord Macaulay, though not himself a Catholic, paid handsome tribute to the Church of Rome:

> The Papacy remains, not in decay, not a mere antique, but full of life and youthful vigor. The Catholic Church is still sending forth to the farthest ends of the world missionaries as zealous as those who landed in Kent with Augustine, and still confronting hostile kings with the same spirit with which she confronted Attila.... She saw the commencement of all the governments and of all the ecclesiastical establishments that now exist in the world.... She was great and respected before the Saxon had set foot on Britain, before the Frank had passed the Rhine, when Grecian eloquence still flourished at Antioch, when idols were still worshipped in the temple of Mecca. And she may still exist in undiminished vigor when some traveller from New Zealand shall, in the midst of a vast solitude, take his stand on a broken arch of London Bridge to sketch the ruins of St. Paul's.

Were Macaulay alive today, he would not have to alter a single word, for this is the Church. This is Catholicism.

Index